First Church of the Brethren
1340 Forge Road
Carlisle, PA 17013-3172

PRAYERS FOR TODAY'S CHURCH

PRAYERS FOR TODAY'S CHURCH

Edited by
DICK WILLIAMS

AUGSBURG PUBLISHING HOUSE
MINNEAPOLIS, MINNESOTA

PRAYERS FOR TODAY'S CHURCH

First United States Edition 1977

Copyright © R. H. L. Williams 1972

First published by CPAS Publications, London

Library of Congress Catalog Card No. 76-27081

International Standard Book No. 0-8066-1565-6

Manufactured in the United States of America

Contents

(Numbers refer to prayers, not pages.)

Prayers for the World

Some Experimental Forms of Worship

Index

Foreword

Because we are human beings, all in need of God, our prayers are never altogether private. Your needs are my needs, and mine are yours. Among the nearly 500 prayers in this book, we will often be startled to find the subjects and words expressing our yearnings so precisely that we may have chosen them ourselves.

The inventory of this book roams the whole range of our common life. *Prayers for Today's Church* is not for lay people alone nor for pastors and church leaders alone, but for everyone.

These crisp, incisive prayers were assembled under the direction of Dick Williams, an Anglican, and come from the hearts and pens of Christians of all ages and from many countries. They were published first in England. The language has both the excellence of the Book of Common Prayer and the contemporary ring of today's newsprint.

The collection falls conveniently into three sections. First are prayers following the majestic tempo of the Christian year. Next are prayers encompassing the vast array of day-to-day needs. Finally, there is a more brief list of what the editor calls experimental forms of worship.

Prayer is always a blend of thanksgiving to God and cries for his mercy and help. This volume is rich in both. Within its scope are intercessions—for governments, for families, for the church, for industry, and for labor. Scattered through the book are special prayers for problem families, for people in prison, for those tempted to suicide, for refugees, for workers in monotonous routines, and for the lonely, the bored, the sick, the dying. The needs of God's great human family in the 20th century—all are included.

These are bracing prayers. They do not give up on people or the world. They breathe faith and hope. They nestle us back into the arms of God; they point us to paths of duty in the world. Offered by today's rank-and-file seekers, they echo universal longings voiced by saints of long ago.

Prayer has always been at the heart of the Christian's life. We were created for God, and God went to the lengths of a cross to recapture us for himself. He is our Father, and we his children. If we had no other need than the need to communicate with him, we would pray, for a father and a child who love one another cherish communicating with each other.

Ours is a day for prayer. Perhaps it has been so in every age. But we live in an anxiety-ridden time. Life-and-death issues loom as dark clouds against the horizon of our future. The complexities of our private, daily lives have also multiplied. We despair of going it alone. We need someone. We need God.

And the lines of communication are open. Christ has opened the way for us. And the Spirit is on hand to guide. We can dial direct at any time, and the line is never busy.

We can pray without words, of course. He understands our sighs, our groans. But each of us urgently yearns to put our wants and desires, our fears and hopes, into words.

From a host of our fellow pilgrims we have words—in this book! To pick up *Prayers for Today's Church* in the morning or at night or any other time and to browse through its pages is to meet the hopes and fears of the human family, the deep stirrings of our own hearts, and the limitless mercies of God.

Alvin N. Rogness

Introduction

'The ideal of "timeless English" is sheer nonsense. No living
language can be timeless. You might as well ask for a
motionless river.'

(C. S. Lewis: *Letters to Malcolm*, p. 14)

Soon after the correspondence columns of the *Church of
England Newspaper* and the *Church Times* carried my request
for contributions to a book of prayers, there was an immediate
and sustained response. Prayers came in from all over Britain,
and from points abroad as distant as Japan. They came from
people of all ages, the youngest being eight, the two oldest
being in their 80s. Most of the prayers came from clergy, but
some came from nurses, teachers, homemakers, people from
the armed forces, and those who, quite naturally, did not
mention their occupations.

The most obvious point proved was that prayer is not a
thing of the past. Christians know that it never can be. But if
sociologists demand evidence, here is a little bit of it—
sufficient to show that prayer is an intense, contemporary
activity.

But its significance is wider still, for nothing can show as
prayer can show the content of people's faith, the range of
interests to which it is applied, and the structure of the
theology which nourishes, and is itself nourished by, that faith.

If one asks people to send whatever they like there is sure
to be great variety in what arrives, but there is no guarantee
the variety will be comprehensive. So it was that while some
prayers were about matters I had not thought much about,
other important themes were completely untouched. When
these gaps became apparent I asked friends to write prayers
designed to fill them. I am very grateful to them for their help.

In thinking about written prayers, no one can afford to

ignore three of the most important influences at work upon
the English language today: newspapers, television and radio.

Newspapers are designed for the eye. Their eye-catching
design is not limited to their use of photographs, for the whole
layout of the writing is designed to catch the attention, to
acquaint the reader immediately with the heart of the article's
message, and to conduct the eye as swiftly as possible through
the main course of whatever report or argument is being
presented.

Television is also, of course, designed for the eye. Anyone
who tape-records a television play and then plays it back is
bound to be impressed by the apparently disconnected nature
of the various speeches which are scattered through long
periods of background music or which appear sporadically
between long tracts of sound effects. In general such
speeches fall flat and unimpressive upon the ear, for the chief
appeal of television is to the eye.

Neither newspaper nor television make their principal entry
into the mind through the ear.

But prayers spoken in public do. And modern prayers are
apt to be modelled more upon the literary patterns of the
newspaper and television than upon those more specifically
designed for the ear.

Radio has mastered the techniques of awakening the whole
mind through sound alone. Record a radio play and compare
it with a recorded television play. The differences leap out
with enormous clarity.

Prayers designed for personal devotional use must take
heed of the newspaper and television design patterns. Prayers
designed for use in church must pay attention to the lessons
of liturgy down the ages, and modernization must be effected
within the canons of good radio, rather than within the canons
of television or the daily press.

But radio, of course, has assimilated into itself excellences
of the other two forms which are appropriate to it. Good
radio mobilizes the whole mind. And this is what a good
prayer must seek to do.

Certainly collecting these prayers has widened my experience,

and, I hope, increased my sensitivity. I have learned that
when I am alone and praying by myself, I am not alone nor
am I praying by myself. And when I am worshipping in a
congregation, that congregation—great or small—is set
among that mighty army which bows the knee to the living
God in the midst of this 'runaway world.'

And all this is fuel for more prayer.

Dick Williams

Prayers for the Christian year

FIRST SUNDAY IN ADVENT

1   O Jesus, risen Lord, who taught us that all mankind will one
day see you as you are, and every man be seen for what he is,
help us and all men everywhere to give to you the lordship
of our life; that in our heart and home, at work and play,
that kingdom which must one day come in power and in
judgment, may dawn in grace and mercy in us now, for your
tender mercy's sake.   Amen.
Dick Williams

2   Jesus, Word of God, you who are the glorious beginning of
our faith and its most glorious end, the one by whom all things
were made, to whom all history moves, Lord of life: help us
to measure the purpose of our lives against the purpose of
your love and to repent; then with mercy rise with healing in
our heart and recreate our inner world, that when we stand
before you at the last we may behold in you our Saviour and
our friend; for your tender mercy's sake.   Amen.
Dick Williams

RETURN OF CHRIST

3   O God, who has given us the sure promise that Jesus will
return to judge the earth: make us ready, we pray, for his
royal coming, that we may consider daily what sort of people
we ought to be, and be found faithful servants waiting and
working for our Master's return. Grant in your mercy that
many may be won for him before he comes, and make us bold
in our witness, that no man's blood may be on our hands on
that day, whether he comes at midnight, or at dawn, or in the
daytime; for his name's sake.   Amen.
Christopher Idle

4   Lord Jesus, we thank you for your promise to return to this
world, not as a tiny baby but as a triumphant king. Keep us
watchful against temptation and joyous in your service, for
your name's sake.   Amen.
M. H. Botting's collection

5   Awaken us Lord, that we may not stand outside your kingdom,
but enter in with thankful hearts.
To you we owe our new names, sons and daughters of God:
Grant that we may think of ourselves as those adopted by
you;
That we may speak with a living message and a sure hope;
That we may live as those with the kingdom of heaven here
in our own hearts;
Through him who is the King, Jesus Christ our Lord.
Amen.
S. C. Casson

6   Forgive us, Lord, that we are not ready for your coming.
We are too busy making money for ourselves – or raising it
for others. Throw out the love of money in our hearts and
lift our eyes in joy to welcome our Redeemer. Even so come
Lord Jesus.   Amen.
Ian D. Bunting

7   **A Sense of History**

Give us, O Lord, a sense of history. Forgive our
preoccupation with the present moment. Teach us to
recognize your hand in the stories of men and nations. Help
us to be thankful for evidence of your loving eye upon our
own lives. Encourage us for the coming days in the knowledge
that your touch has still its ancient power; through Jesus
Christ our Lord.
Ian D. Bunting

THE SECOND SUNDAY IN ADVENT

8   Grant, O Lord, that in the written Word, and through the
spoken word, we may behold the living Word, our Saviour
Jesus Christ.   Amen.
Simon H. Baynes

9   Lord God, you have given us the Bible as a lamp and a light.
Let this light not be dimmed by obscure words, and let our
eyes not be dimmed by pride. Help us to understand your
message and its medium, and by your Holy Spirit bring us to
the truth, through Jesus Christ our Lord.   Amen.
after R. C. Thorp

10   Father we thank you for the Bible, because rich and poor,
wise and simple, old and young, sad and happy, can find in it
the answer to their needs. We pray that it will continue to be
translated into the tongues men speak, so that all may know
that you came to us in Christ; for his name's sake.   Amen.
after Patricia Mitchell

11   Heavenly Father, you have shown the wonder of your love
for us in Jesus Christ through the Bible. Help us to
understand it with our minds and apply it in our lives, for his
name's sake.   Amen.
M. H. Botting's collection

12   Thank you, Lord, for the Bible: for its ability to give us each
day new vision and new power; for its capacity to reach to
the roots of our inner life and to refresh them; for its power
to enter into the innermost structures of mind and spirit and
fashion them anew. For the Bible, and its power to beget
faith and to sustain it, we give you thanks and praise; through
Jesus Christ our Saviour.   Amen.
Dick Williams

13   O God of love, and thought, and speech, we thank you for
making man in your own image that he too may love, and

think, and speak, and in his humanity learn to hear your voice
and to reply. We thank you for the many ways you have
revealed your mind and declared your counsel to the hearts of
men. In particular we thank you for the holy Scriptures in
which we learn all we need to know of your love for men
and your purpose for history. Help us so to know your Word
that we may understand it and so to love it that we may obey
it, and so to obey it that we may cause it to be heard, loved,
and obeyed throughout creation; for the sake of Jesus Christ
our Lord. Amen.
Dick Williams

14 O God, whose Word is life, we ask you to bless those who
cannot hear that Word and so are denied its life. Move the
hearts of Christian people everywhere to right this wrong by
setting forward the work of translating and publishing the
holy Scriptures, and preaching their good news. Call to this
enterprise those best equipped to do it. Call us all to support
it. And grant that by the labours of everyone and the blessing
of your spirit, your Word may come with great clarity and
great power into all the world for its salvation, through
Jesus Christ our Lord. Amen.
Dick Williams

15 The Law

O Lord we praise you for the signposts in life which point us
to the highway of your love and purpose. We thank you for
the witness of your creation. We thank you for your law
revealed to Moses. We thank you for the Lord Jesus Christ
who fulfils that law. May we read it as those who search for
the truth and obey it as those who find the truth; for Jesus'
sake.
Ian D. Bunting

16 The Written Word

We thank you Lord for those little pleasures of each day
which are ours through the written word – the newspapers,
the women's magazine, the letter from a friend. Help us to

remember those who cannot read. Guard us from those who
would pervert our minds or poison our souls. Direct those
who write and, above all, open our eyes to the truth of your
Word; through Jesus Christ our Lord.
Ian D. Bunting

An Act of Praise for the Bible

17   Let us give thanks to God.
Praise the Lord, O my soul;
And all that is within me praise his holy name.
Praise the Lord, O my soul;
And forget not all his benefits.
Let God be thanked that he has given us his message
written in the Law and the Prophets, in the wisdom of the
Proverbs and the poetry of the Psalms,
above all in the Gospel of our Lord Jesus Christ, the Word
made flesh.
Thanks be to God.
Let God be thanked for the Bible in English; for those who
long ago gave us early translations; for those who down the
years improved them, enabling the Scriptures to penetrate
deeply into our national language and life.
Thanks be to God.
Let God be thanked that in our ever-changing language the
work of translation continues, and for all that the Bible
means to so many in the churches and the homes of the English
speaking world.
Thanks be to God.
Let God be thanked for those who translate, publish and
distribute in other languages, so that all men may come to the
knowledge of the gospel.
Thanks be to God.
Let us sum up our prayers in the prayer that Christ has
taught us.
Our Father...
J. Meirion Lloyd

18   Feed the Minds: A Meditation and Prayer

Let us in God's presence reflect upon the power of the
printed word:
The printed word can give new thoughts and ideas to millions
of readers;
it can survive to speak across the centuries;
it can reach those who are cut off from the influence of the
spoken word;
it can speak intimately to people in their own homes;
it can be left behind to continue its message when the spoken
word is silenced.

But the printed word can be either poison or food; it can
propagate lies, suspicion, and hatred – or truth, trust and
friendship.
So we pray for those who are now learning to read, that their
new skill may become for them a means of knowing and
loving our Lord Jesus Christ.
O Lord, hear our prayer;
And let our cry come unto thee.

We pray also for those who teach the illiterate to read, and
we remember before God
writers and translators;
journalists and artists;
printers, publishers, and booksellers;
that they may make wise and responsible use of this power of
moulding the minds of men.
O Lord, hear our prayer;
And let our cry come unto thee.

With thanksgiving to God for what we have been enabled to
do in the past, let us offer to him ourselves, our gifts, our
possessions, in proclaiming the good news of the Christian
gospel by means of the printed word through the great
literature societies long dedicated to their task;
O Lord, hear our prayer;
And let our cry come unto thee.

Liverpool Cathedral

THIRD SUNDAY IN ADVENT

19   Thank you, Father, for every messenger of yours, who stands
unbowed in the godless spirit of our age. Thank you for those
who stand up for justice and truth before their own rights
and freedom. May their example inspire us to the same
faithfulness to Jesus Christ our Lord.   Amen.
Ian D. Bunting

THE MINISTRY
20   **A Prayer for the Ministry**

O Jesus, true God and true man, bless those whom you call
to the work of the Christian ministry.
Help them to hear your call, help them to obey it;
provide them abundantly with the necessities of life, save
them from love of luxury;
make them ambitious to do your will, save them from
worldly ambitions;
give them the powers of a united mind, save them from a
divided heart;
sustain them in their desire to give to you the whole of their
life;
help them to measure their gift against the glory of your love
and the depth of eternity;
deepen and enlarge their knowledge of their calling, save them
from cynicism, weariness and despair;
help them so to possess the riches of the world to come, that
they may attain to true humanity in this;
and inspire them so to speak your word that all mankind
might receive it, believe it and obey it;
through Jesus Christ our Lord.   Amen.
Dick Williams

21   **Those called to the Ministry**

We thank you God for making man in such a way that what
he is can respond to what you are: bless all those whose
response to your call takes the form of service in the sacred
ministry; make perfect their desire to be your servants;

increase their understanding of man's need and your great
love: so may they find power, peace and gladness and share
the same with those whom they shall serve; through Jesus
Christ our Minister and our Lord.   Amen.
Dick Williams

22   Theological Seminaries

Raise up in the Church, O Lord, persons of faith and vision
to be our leaders. Be with all who teach and all who learn in
our seminaries; that we may receive persons for the ministry
who are spirit-filled teachers and leaders who command
respect. We pray in the name of the Good Shepherd, Jesus
Christ our Lord. Amen.
Ian D. Bunting

23

Almighty God, Father of Jesus, giver of life, teacher of all:
bless the work of all theological seminaries; guide those who
regulate their affairs; instruct those who teach; discipline (that
is, make disciples of) those who learn; and grant that all may
discover the nature of their needs and the scale of your powers.
Give to each seminary a rich and happy inner life in which
diversity of minds, through unity of spirit, may glorify Christ,
for the worth of his name and the spread of his kingdom.
Amen.
Dick Williams

24   Retired Clergy

O Lord Jesus Christ, who on Calvary offered your finished
work to the Father; look upon all clergy who have retired or
who, for other reasons, have offered back their ministries to
you. Grant them your peace, that their faith may be
strengthened and their love of you increased until they come
at last unto your everlasting kingdom, O Saviour, who with
the Father and the Holy Spirit lives and reigns for ever and
ever.   Amen.
Andrew Warner

FOURTH SUNDAY IN ADVENT

25   Teach us, Lord, the humility of true servants. When we want
to be noticed, remind us of men like John the Baptist.
Forgive the way we use people to our own ends. Lead us to
that place where we become no more than a voice for you to
use, to your glory, through Jesus Christ our Lord.   Amen.
Ian D. Bunting

26   **The Dying Thief**

We leave so much to the last minute. Yet even then, Father,
you would meet us. Forgive us the sins we had no time to
think about or confess. At this moment our lives lie open to
you like a book. You have paid our debts: we can call only
upon your love; through Jesus Christ our Lord.   Amen.
Ian D. Bunting

27   **Men of Destiny**

Thank you Father that in the fullness of time you sent your
Son to be our Saviour. We believe that in the fullness of time
he will be coming to be our king. Set alight the spark of hope
and confidence in our hearts, that we may live as those who
have a certain goal, in Jesus Christ our Lord.   Amen.
Ian D. Bunting

CHRISTMAS

28   **A Homemaker's Prayer Before Christmas**

It has begun. The hurly-burly of preparations; the making of
cakes and puddings; the aching hands and feet; the anxious
search for presents.
Is this as it should be, Lord?
Father we call a halt. Here, and now, and at this moment.
And we think of the first Christmas when history paused and
turned upon its hinges as your Son became a man, born into
the family of a working man, born to experience everything
for us – and even to bear our sin.
Help each one of us to prepare for Christmas by finding time
for quiet, time to drink in the wonder and beauty of your
Son's birth, time to offer again our hearts and each part of our
life to him.

May the pages of our diary turn upon this silent hinge. May
our work be rooted and grounded in peace.
Lord hear our prayer: and give your grace.
Jesus said 'My peace I give to you, but not the sort the
world gives.'
Father we understand only too well the kind of peace which
mankind manufactures: the peace of political and other
settlements. Give to more and more of us all over the world,
the peace we do not understand, the peace which passes
understanding, the peace which flows from unconditional
obedience to the law of love, give us your kind of peace.
And we pray for those in positions of power, authority and
influence, that they may open their hearts and give their wills
to you, that you may work through them.
Lord hear our prayer: and give your grace.
Jesus said: 'When you give food or drink to someone who
hasn't got any, you're giving it to me.'
Save us, Father, from becoming hardened to the numerous
pleas for help we see in the press each day. Open our eyes and
our pockets to the needs of the world around us. Reorganize
our hearts so that it may not be a burden to give but a relief.
Lord hear our prayer: and give your grace.
Jesus said: 'Man cannot live by bread alone.'
Dear Lord, the giver of all, guide our giving so that we may
support all those who spend their lives, at home and all over
the world, feeding the spirit of man with the good news of
Christmas.
Lord hear our prayer: and give your grace.
Father, with all our hearts we thank you for all that you have
given us through Jesus Christ our Lord.   Amen.
after Patricia Mitchell

29   May our homes be homes of peace and love at Christmas:
Because we plan carefully,
Prepare well,
And give as Jesus gives
To make it all come true.
J. E. Morris

30 O God, we shall be very busy over Christmas, and we know that we shall be tempted to forget the true meaning of this festival. Help us to conquer that temptation so that we may share with our families the true joy of the Saviour's birth, for his name's sake. Amen.
Andrew Warner

31 **Christmas**

O God, our Father, as we remember the birth of your Son, Jesus Christ, we welcome him with gladness as Saviour and pray that there may always be room for him in our hearts and in our homes, for his sake. Amen.
M. H. Botting's collection

32 O Holy Spirit of Christ, Teacher, Helper, and Friend;
Open the hearts and minds of many this Christmas time to the good and saving news of Jesus Christ; that those who are insecure, or empty, or aimless, may find in the one from Bethlehem all that they need today, and much more besides. For his name's sake. Amen.

33 O God our Father, we pray that you will bless every baby born at Christmas time; their mothers, their families, their homes. May they receive a better welcome from our world than Jesus did; and may they come to know him as their Saviour and Friend. For his sake. Amen.
Christopher Idle

34 Almighty Father, who by the glorious incarnation of your Son Jesus Christ, has sent a new light into the world; give us grace that we may so receive the same light into our hearts as to be guided by it into the way of everlasting salvation; through the same Jesus Christ our Lord. Amen.
Piers Nash-Williams

35 Christ, born in a stable, give courage to the homeless.
Christ who fled to Egypt, comfort the refugee.
Christ who fasted in the desert, have mercy on the hungry.
Christ who hung in torture on the cross, pity those in pain.

Christ who died to save us, above all forgive our sin, our
greed, our selfishness, our unconcern.
Save us today and use us in your loving purposes.
Simon H. Baynes

36   Jesus – who to us is the expression of what God is and of
what God does, help us to get our thinking straight about
Christmas. May we see it not just as a fairy tale from the past
but as possessing great truths for our world today.
Jesus – born in a stable, may we honour you by serving those
who are homeless now.
Jesus – a refugee in Egypt, may our concern for today's
refugees be part of our worship to you.
Jesus – bringer of peace, may our striving for peace in the
world be part of our Christmas offering to you.
Jesus – who received gifts from men, help us to give ourselves
to you: that you may make us the kind of people you want us
to be: that you may show us the kind of life you want us to
lead.
Jesus – who gave all for us, accept our lives and set them on
fire with love for you and for all mankind.
We ask this in your name and for your sake, Jesus Christ our
Lord.   Amen.
Gordon Bates

37   A Bidding Prayer

Let us pray for the Church: that it may be as humble, as
relevant, and as mighty as the Lord who was born of Mary.

Let us pray for the world in all its splendour and need, in all
its grief and its glory: that it may look to God for help.

Let us pray that as God stirred the Wise Men to follow their
star and find the Christ, so may we, and all mankind, be
stirred to seek for the truth and to find the Saviour.

And as God opened the heavens and summoned the
shepherds, let us pray that we and all men everywhere
might look for God's Word, and at its coming rise up and go
where God shall direct.

And as God prepared Mary to be the Mother of Jesus let us
ask God to prepare our hearts, and the hearts of all people, to
receive the Lord of Glory: that in this glad and solemn season
each heart might be a manger and each home a Bethlehem.
Dick Williams

38   Before a Carol Service

Lord, we've sung these carols and heard this story so many
times before. We confess that we have allowed the most
important event in history to become dulled by familiarity.
Help us in this act of worship to recapture a sense of wonder.
Let us discover with surprise the stupendous fact that the
Creator of the universe has shown himself in a new born child.
Enable us to accept what we shall never fully understand. So
may we worship with a genuine joy.   Amen.
J. D. Searle

CHILDREN'S PRAYERS FOR CHRISTMAS

39   Let us thank God for Christmas:
For this happy and exciting time of the year
  Thank you loving Father.
For Christmas trees and decorations
  Thank you loving Father.
For cards and presents and good food
  Thank you loving Father.
For fun with family and friends
  Thank you loving Father.
For singing carols and listening to the Christmas story
  Thank you loving Father.
For all these things because we have them to remind us of the
coming of Jesus
  Thank you loving Father.
J. D. Searle

40   Let us remember those who do not have the things that make us happy. In the short times of quiet, we shall think of people we may know. Then I will say the words: 'As we remember them' and every one will reply, *Help them loving Father*.
We remember this Christmas:
Those who are sad or lonely.
(*Silence*.)
As we remember them:
    Help them loving Father.
Those who are ill or handicapped:
(*Silence*.)
As we remember them:
    Help them loving Father.
Those who are poor or hungry:
(*Silence*.)
As we remember them:
    Help them loving Father.
Those who are old or unwanted:
(*Silence*.)
As we remember them:
    Help them loving Father.
Heavenly Father, show us ways in which we may help those for whom we have prayed; for the sake of Jesus Christ. Amen.
J. D. Searle

41   **Christmas Prayers for Children's Services**

We thank you, Heavenly Father, for sending your only Son, Jesus Christ, to become part of the family of man. We thank you for Mary and Joseph who looked after him and guarded and protected him when he was little. We thank you for bringing him to manhood so that in all his earthly life we can see what you are like. We thank you for reminding us at Christmas how much you love us, and for helping us to realize that you always have loved us and always will. Help us to love and serve you gladly in return, through Jesus Christ our Lord.   Amen.
Dick Williams

42   Almighty God, who sent Jesus to be the Saviour of mankind,
      we pray for all the peoples of the world. Because Jesus was
      born for all, may he be welcomed by all, and may the love he
      came to bring strengthen and inspire those who work to
      spread his kingdom, for his name's sake.   Amen.
      Dick Williams

43   We pray, O Lord, for all the children in the world who do
      not have homes; those who are hungry, sick or sad; all
      children in hospital, and all whose parents are sick. Bless
      them and everybody else who is in trouble, and help us all to
      work together to make them well and happy again, through
      the help of your grace and power, given to the world through
      Jesus Christ our Lord.   Amen.
      Dick Williams

EPIPHANY

44   Lord God, we remember how you led the wise men to
      Bethlehem by the light of a star. Guide us as we travel to the
      heavenly city that we and all men may know Jesus as the true
      and living way, for his name's sake.   Amen.
      M. H. Botting's collection

45   **Christian Missions, Home and Overseas**

      O Lord, we are called to be your witnesses. Help us to make
      Jesus our Saviour known to others through our words and
      our lives, our prayers and our gifts, for your sake.   Amen.
      M. H. Botting's collection

46   Heavenly Father, we pray for those who have gone to other
      countries with good news of Jesus.
      When their work is difficult and tiring make them strong;
      when they are lonely and homesick remind them that you are
      with them; when they are uncertain what to do, guide them,
      and keep them at all times loving you, for Jesus' sake.
      Amen.
      M. H. Botting's collection

NEW YEAR

47 **Watch Night**

Look upon us tonight, Lord, as we pray to you, with our
tiny resolutions and enormous fears; our tiny achievements
and enormous failings; our tiny vision and enormous tasks.
Be with those who are very conscious of the vanity and
frustration of this world, and show them that Christ makes all
things new. Be with those also who do not feel this
frustration; be with the self-satisfied, the rich, the proud and
the powerful, that they may see in Christ a much more
excellent way.

Look upon our homes and families and dear ones; those
from whom we are separated, those for whom we are
anxious, those with whom we have quarrelled. Bring into
every human relationship the unity and healing and strength
of your Son.

Look upon our church in all its needs. Come among us in
refreshing and reviving power in this coming year.

Look upon our world with all its waste and war and sorrow,
and all its joys as well; and make your believing people more
effective in serving it, in bringing it light, and in sharing with
it the fragrance of Christ.
All these things we ask for the honour of his name.
Christopher Idle

48 **At the End of One Year and the Beginning of Another**

Lord of time and new beginnings, give us good judgment to
know what new things to do for you this year, and grant us
the inner strength to finish each job we begin; so may we
fully know the joy of doing your will; so may your kingdom
come on earth; through Jesus Christ our Lord.   Amen.
Susan Williams

49 Help us, O Lord, to enter this new year as your people of old
entered their promised land: give us, like them, a sense of
vocation; give us, like them, the promise of your presence:
so may this year, in all its possibilities for good and ill, be

lived with power, in fellowship with you, in harmony of
spirit, and for the good of all mankind: through Jesus Christ
our Lord.   Amen.
Dick Williams

50   Grant Lord, that as the years change we may find rest in your
eternal changelessness. May we go forward into this year
with courage, sure in the faith that while life changes around
us, you are always the same, guiding us with your wisdom and
protecting us with your love. So may the peace which passes
understanding keep our hearts and minds in Christ Jesus, and
your blessing be upon all nations and upon all whom we
love, in the name of the Father, and of the Son and of the
Holy Spirit.   Amen.
Harold E. Evans

51   **Stewardship at the Start of a New Year**

Jesus gave his disciples plenty of practical advice for living
in a hard world. Here is one of the things he said: 'Give and
it will be given to you; good measure, pressed down, shaken
together, running over, will men put into your lap.'
As we plan for the new year let us meditate on the Lord's
advice.

I've started a new year Lord.
Only (14) (*or whatever the number*) days have gone, and I've
been extravagant saving money at the sales.
Only (14) days have gone and we're planning the summer
holidays.
Only (14) days have gone, and I'm thankful the kids are back
at school.

Going back to what you said, Lord,
I don't think your first disciples had a very high standard of
living.
And yet you said 'Give'...
Give what?
The same things I suppose that were given to me:
my time...my friendship...my money...my love...my life...

I love the glorious extravagance of your promise, Lord. As I
give, so will I be richly rewarded in return.

It's a new year, Lord, and I'm working out a budget of what
I want to give in service to you;
In tens and hundreds,
in time and talents,
in loving and living.
And I know, whatever the cost, you'll give me back a
hundredfold.
Thank you.   Amen.
Patricia Mitchell

52   An Act of Praise

Let us give thanks to God for our own creation:
I am fearfully and wonderfully made:
And that my soul knoweth right well.
For my birth and life:
 I praise you, O God.
For the strength of my body, its resistance to disease, and its
power of recovery:
 I praise you, O God.
For the workings of my hands:
 I praise you, O God.
For the journeyings of my feet:
 I praise you, O God.
For the seeing of my eyes and the hearing of my ears:
 I praise you, O God.
For the sight of beauty in nature and in art:
 I praise you, O God.
For the interest and joy of reading:
 I praise you, O God.
For the meaning and beauty of words:
 I praise you, O God.
And the melodies and harmonies of music:
 I praise you, O God.
For the efficient working of my brain:
 I praise you, O God.

For the power of mind and thought:
I praise you, O God.
For the sensitivity and strength of feeling:
I praise you, O God.
For the sense of conscience:
I praise you, O God.
For the gift of will:
I praise you, O God.
For my inner self, its hidden nature, its name known only to you:
I praise you, O God.
For its need of you, its consciousness of thee, its communion with you:
I praise you, O God.
For its hope of eternal life, through your Son Jesus Christ:
I praise you, O God.
Liverpool Cathedral

53   Creation

Lord, you have created man in your own image to enjoy the fullness of life that comes from fellowship with you. We praise you for the dignity and nobility that you have bestowed upon man. We praise you for his many achievements in art, literature, medicine, exploration, science, architecture and technology. Yet we confess that men have disgraced your gifts through war, prejudice, hatred, power-seeking and unconcern. Forgive our abuse of your gifts, our failure to conform to your will. Grant that, through your Holy Spirit, we may fulfil our potential as you require us to do and, in communion with you, be transformed in the life and into likeness of your Son Jesus Christ, who is the very glory of man, and in whose name we pray.   Amen.
Alan Nugent

54   Lord of the universe, we praise you for your creation; the wonder of space, the beauty of the world and the value of earth's resources. Keep us from spoiling them by our

selfishness and help us to use them for the good of all men and the glory of your name.   Amen.
M. H. Botting's collection

55   We praise you God almighty for the power you have shown in creating the world. We thank you for your love in redeeming us from sin, and creating us anew in Christ. Grant us strength in this life to honour you, Lord God, both in worship and in witness, for Jesus Christ's sake.   Amen.
R. C. Thorp

56   **Flowers**

Father, we cannot grow a flower, paint its petals or give it perfume. Yet day by day we become more self-sufficient and less thankful for your goodness in creation. Give us grateful hearts for every mercy and most of all for Jesus Christ our Lord.
Ian D. Bunting

57   **Spring**

We thank you, Heavenly Father, for every sign of Spring which we see in the world around us. Above all we thank you for the rising again of Jesus Christ which announces to the world the dawn of new light and life and hope. May it be springtime in our hearts and lives, that the new life of Christ within us may inspire us to serve you faithfully in our daily lives; for the sake of Jesus Christ our Lord.   Amen.
Ian D. Bunting

LENT
58   **A Meditation for Ash Wednesday**

Help us, O Lord, to fix our minds on the sufferings and temptations of Jesus Christ.

Help us to see him far from home and friends, enduring the trial of his manhood. Help us to see him tortured by hunger, yet not using miraculous powers for selfish ends; desiring the subjection of the world to his father's will, yet refusing to give honour to the devil; longing to open the eyes of men and women to his glory, yet not stooping to sensational means.

Help us to look steadily at him, who suffered such things for us. Help us to behold his great love. Help us to see his sinless perfection.

When we are in pain or sickness, grief or sorrow, fear or anxiety, help us to turn to him who bore not only pain but also the weight and burden of our sins.

When we seek to conquer sin and bring our lives back into the true and narrow way, help us to turn to him.

At the beginning of this season of Lent, help us now to turn to him.

Holy Jesus, sufferer, sin-bearer: take our hearts and purify them; take our lives and reform them; take all we are this Lent and make us more like you, for your name's sake.
Simon H. Baynes

59   Homemaker's Meditation for Lent

'Jesus returned from the Jordan...and was led by the Holy Spirit to spend 40 days in the desert...'

Lord it is Lent:
the time when some people give up luxuries in order to assume new duties.
The time when some people do their Spring cleaning, and buy new clothes for Easter.
But what did you do Lord to make this season what it is?
You got away from people: away from the distracting things of daily life, because you wanted to listen to your Father and find his way to conquer evil and liberate your friends.
Then you returned and met life at the points where good and evil meet, and everybody saw the power of God in you.

So what do I do Lord in this restless age?
The terrible temptation is to rush around every day being busy.

There is a terrible temptation to think I can't find time for
quiet, or even find a quiet place.
But in my heart of hearts I know that I need you.
Now in this age of jet-propulsion, space research and
automation,
I must make time and find a place: a time and a place to learn
the art of listening, Lord, and get to know you better.

That's what I'll do this Lent, Lord.
Patricia Mitchell

60   Patience in Seeking God's Will

'Jesus, after he had fasted forty days and forty nights...was
hungry.'
Lord we are hungry for the knowledge of the next step we
must take. Give to us the long patience of Christ that we, like
him, may not decide our future in haste; mercifully grant that
hunger for an improvement in our lot; hunger for release
from tension or anxiety; hunger for success in your service;
or any other kind of appetite for things hidden in the future
may not stampede the soul into premature decisions.
Instead of turning the stones of impatience into the bread of
hasty action, may it be our meat and drink to do your will,
and like the Saviour find that we have meat to eat we knew
not of.
Make us not to hunger for tomorrow, but to hunger and thirst
after righteousness, in the sure knowledge that they who do
so shall be filled; through Jesus Christ our Lord.   Amen.
Dick Williams

61   A Prayer for Guidance

Help us, Lord, to think about our life as Jesus thought about
his:
Help us to understand the nature of our calling;
the nature of the One who calls;
the nature of the world's needs;
the nature of our own resources;
the nature of God's provision.

Help us not to drift through life but to seek your guidance.
Save us from making hasty decisions; save us from making
no decisions at all.
Help us to seek not our own glory but yours.
Help us to have no ambition but to do good.
Make us pure in heart.
And help us, finally, not to judge ourselves, and not to judge
others but to leave judgment where it belongs
with him to whom all power is given,
the one who knows all and loves each,
Jesus Christ our Saviour and our Lord.   Amen.
Dick Williams

62   Victory Against Temptation

O Lord Jesus Christ, who, as man, knew the weakness of our
nature and the power of temptation, but who overcame all
things by the grace of God, so breathe into our hearts the
strength of your spirit and clothe us with heavenly armour,
that we may conquer all that wars against our souls and may
be kept your faithful soldiers and servants to the end.   Amen.
Harold E. Evans

63   Holiness

Lord Jesus, help us to pray. Increase our faith, that no
problem we face may be too big for us to overcome. Help us
to see that by keeping us on our knees you are strengthening
our trust and obedience in your purposes, through Jesus
Christ our Lord.   Amen.
Joyce Francis

CHILDREN'S PRAYERS FOR LENT
64   Grace to Confess

O God you made us and you love us; thank you for being so
willing to forgive us. Make us quick to own up to you
whenever we do wrong so that we may quickly be forgiven.
Then our day will not be spoilt by worry and we can be happy
all day long, through Jesus Christ our Lord.   Amen.
Dick Williams

65   Fasting

O Lord Jesus, thank you for fasting forty days and forty
nights in order to help us. Teach us how to train our bodies
to serve our wills, and may it always be our will to be your
servants, for your dear name's sake.   Amen.
Dick Williams

66   First Sunday in Lent

'Jesus was then led away by the Spirit into the wilderness, to
be tempted by the devil' (Matthew 4).

O Lord, who has sent us out into all the world to make
followers from every nation, help us to resist the
temptations which you yourself have conquered. Keep us
from offering to the hungry nothing but bread; from
presenting proofs instead of a Person; and from serving the
forces of this world in the hope that they will serve us, your
messengers; through the power of your name.   Amen.
Susan Williams

67   O Lord, who was tested with a choice of three ways to do
your work, help us in our own lives always to choose the
fourth way, the way of suffering and of the Cross.   Amen.
Susan Williams

68   Second Sunday in Lent

'A Canaanite woman...came crying out, "Sir! have pity...
My daughter is tormented..." ' (Matthew 15.22).

O Lord, when those we love are attacked by evil, help us
never to give up the search for grace and healing, but to
spend our lives following you and trusting in your love and
power.   Amen.
Susan Williams

69 O Lord of all men, sent to your own people but exposed to pressures from strangers, help us when we face demands which lie beyond our limits. Grant us the vision which sees the expanding task, and the strength which is able to carry it out, to the glory of your name.   Amen.
Susan Williams

70 O Lord, you found faith in unexpected people, in people scorned by the religious men of your time. Help us to live in your Church so close to those outside it, that we may know and share true faith across the border.   Amen.
Susan Williams

71 **Third Sunday in Lent**

'If it is by the finger of God that I drive out the devils, then be sure that the kingdom of God has already come upon you' (Luke 11.20).

O Lord, whose love has brought us to know you, and whose power drives out the evil inside us, help us to fill our lives with obedience to your will, so that your indwelling may be complete, and evil find no home in our hearts; through the power of your Spirit.   Amen.
Susan Williams

72 O Lord, whose power to heal was tested against the power which destroys, and proved stronger: open our eyes to the signs of your strength in this modern world, and open our hearts to the Kingdom of God, which has come upon us; through the power of your Spirit.   Amen.
Susan Williams

73 **Fourth Sunday in Lent**

'Then Jesus took the loaves, gave thanks and distributed them to the people...' (John 6.11).

O Lord, who used the gift of one to fill the need of thousands, help us so to care for others that without shame

or despair we may offer you all we have, to the glory of your
name.   Amen.
Susan Williams

74   O Lord, who healed the sick and fed the healthy, who knows
and meets all our needs: keep us from following you merely
for the joy and strength you offer, and help us in love to take
the way of the Cross, for your name's sake.   Amen.
Susan Williams

75   **Fifth Sunday in Lent**

'Jesus said, "Before Abraham was born, I am". They picked
up stones to throw at him...' (John 8.58–59).

O Lord, who came to show God to men and was not afraid
of their anger, take from us the wish to speak in inoffensive
whispers in an unwelcoming world, and make us strong to
speak of you boldly; in your name.   Amen.
Susan Williams

76   O Lord of time, Lord from before our birth to beyond our
death; help us to know you in each moment, so that, keeping
your word, we may live now in the free and greater life of
God.   Amen.
Susan Williams

77   **Palm Sunday**

'Jesus then went into the Temple and drove out all who were
buying and selling' (Matthew 21.12).

O Lord, who drove from the temple those whose aim it was
to make money, drive from our hearts the desire to own
things and to do well in this life. May we, who are your
Church and Temple, be filled with you alone, so that we may
show your glory to the world and in your name heal.   Amen.
Susan Williams

78   O Lord, who rode straight into the power of the enemy to
suffer and die, give us the strength to follow you to the

centres of opposition in this world, and the confidence which
confronts power with love.   Amen.
Susan Williams

79   O God of grace and love, in thankfulness for all that you have
given us through the loving care and hard work of *our*
mothers, we pray for your richest blessing upon *all*
mothers:
For those with difficult homes, whose children are more of a
problem than a blessing;
For those with difficult husbands, who find it hard to be
constant and loving;
For those with loved ones far away, and those who are
lonely;
For those who find it hard to make ends meet, or who go short
themselves for the sake of their families;
For those who are nearly at the end of their tether;
For those mothers who are trying to make Christ real to their
families;
For those who do not know him as their Saviour, nor how to
cast their care on him;
For each one according to her need, hear our prayer, and
draw all mothers closer to you today, through your son
Jesus Christ our Lord.
Christopher Idle

80   A Prayer for Mothers

Loving God, we thank you that Jesus enjoyed a mother's
love and grew up within a family.
We thank you for the homes where we were born and for
the care and affection of *our* mothers.
We thank you if we are still privileged to enjoy the warmth
and security of family life.
We pray for all mothers today:
For expectant mothers, especially those awaiting the birth of
their first child;

For those who have young children and who get tired and
harassed with so much to do;
For those who are anxious because their children are
growing up and seem to be growing away from them;
For those who feel a sense of emptiness as their children
marry and leave home;
For those who are elderly and may feel unwanted;
For those who have no husband to share their responsibilities
– the widowed, the divorced and the unmarried mother.
We pray also for:
Those who have been denied the privilege of motherhood –
those who cannot have children of their own, and those who
have never had the opportunity to marry.

Lastly, we pray for those closest to us; may we love and care
for them as we ourselves have been loved and helped. We ask
it for your love's sake.   Amen.
John D. Searle

81   Remember, O Lord, all those in need;
People with no good food or proper clothes;
No home of their own or no work to do;
No family or friends, or no knowledge of your love.
Supply their needs; bless those who try to help them; and
bring them all to trust in you.   Amen.
Christopher Idle

82   We thank you, heavenly Father, for our friends and families;
May your love surround them;
May your strength protect them;
May your truth guide them;
That we may love one another very much, and love you with
all our hearts, and best of all; for Jesus' sake.   Amen.
Christopher Idle

83   We pray to you, O God, that those of us who are husbands
or wives may love and serve each other;
That those of us who are fathers or mothers may be fair and
kind to our children;

That those of us who are sons or daughters may obey and help
our parents;
That those of us who are brothers or sisters may share
willingly and give generously;
And that all of us may grow daily more like Jesus Christ,
who once gave himself for us, and is now the best friend of
every family; for his name's sake.   Amen.
Christopher Idle

84   As people who belong to God
        We must be patient, humble and kind.
    Forbearing and forgiving one another
        As the Lord has forgiven us.
    Above all we must have love
        Which binds us together in harmony.
    Let the peace of Christ rule our lives
        As we join in worshipping him.
    Our songs and hymns are full of praise
        Giving thanks to God through Christ.
    Our work and service is whole hearted
        Not just for one another but for Christ.
    So that in every word and deed
        Our aim is to please and honour him.
    Christopher Idle

85   Children's Prayer for Mothers

    Loving God, thank you for our homes and for family life.
    Today we thank you especially for the love and care of our
    mothers.
    If we have no mother of our own, we thank you for whoever
    takes her place.
    We thank you that she cooks our meals, cleans the house and
    mends our clothes.
    We thank you that she corrects us when we are naughty and
    cheers us up when we feel sad.
    We are sorry if we forget that housework can make her tired.
    We are sorry if our carelessness causes her extra work.

We are sorry if we sometimes seem to be ungrateful for all
that she does for us.
Help us to be more thoughtful, helpful and kind at home.
Through Jesus Christ. Amen.
John D. Searle

86   Children's Prayer for Fathers

Loving God, there are so many things for which we are
grateful.
We are especially thankful today for our fathers.
We thank you for their love, care and protection.
We thank you that they work to earn money to buy us food
and clothes and all we need.
We thank you that they play with us and take us on holiday.
We remember those who have no father and ask that there
may be someone who will look after them and make them
happy.
Lord, we are glad to remember that Jesus taught us that we
can call you 'Father'.
Help us to try to please you as well. Amen.
John D. Searle

PRAYERS FOR HOLY WEEK
87   The Crowd

Have mercy, O Lord, on all those whose judgment of truth is
rooted in the opinions of others; all who are swayed by
pressure groups to do deeds which they themselves would
never think of doing; all whose lack of purpose, lack of
conviction, lack of stability or lack of employment, makes
them available to the purposes of others and delivers them as
a weapon into the hands of evil men: give to all people
everywhere, O Lord, a spirit of responsibility and discernment,
and make them more ready to seek for the truth and less
ready to believe a lie; through Jesus Christ our Lord. Amen.
Dick Williams

88   The High Priest

Have mercy, O Lord, on all who bear high office and abuse
its authority; all who plot courses of political action for the
sole purpose of protecting their own positions; all who
persecute prophets because of the evil they expose; all who
manufacture a lie for public consumption; all who treat
prophets and public alike as pawns and puppets: on all such,
everywhere, O Lord, have mercy. Help them to worship
truth, and to give God the glory. Teach them to know and to
understand, to believe and to trust, that for the mighty as for
the meek it is only by losing our life that we find it, only by
dying that we live; only by following Christ that we lead
men; for his name's sake.   Amen.
Dick Williams

89   Pilate

Have mercy, O Lord, on all who are called to the terrible
loneliness of giving judgment; all who know that upon their
conclusions rest the lives of others; all who are the object of
bribery or menace. Give them great courage and great
goodness. Make them wise in heart, humble in spirit, accurate
in thought, brave in decision, resolute in life. Make them
righteous and give them peace, through Jesus Christ our
Lord.   Amen.
Dick Williams

90   Frightened Disciples

O God, who knows our weakness, have mercy on us and all
Christian people when we are tempted to cast away our
confidence in Christ. When the high and mighty are against
him, and when the crowd cries for his blood, help us to cling
to his cross and behold his face. And as you saved and
delivered the first disciples, so, by the power of the
resurrection, save and deliver us too, we pray, through the
same Jesus Christ our Lord.   Amen.
Dick Williams

91   Barabbas

Have mercy, O Lord, on all who have killed and robbed and
destroyed, but go unpunished. Turn their hearts, O Lord,
and help them to repent. By the wounds of Christ save them
from the wounds of fruitless remorse. Give them instead that
godly sorrow which leads to life. And may lives which have
been slaves of evil become servants of love, through Jesus
Christ our Lord.   Amen.
Dick Williams

92   Joseph of Arimathea

Bless all, O Lord, who worship you in secret; all whose
hearts are growing round an undeclared allegiance; all whose
life is laden with a treasure they would pour out at your feet;
all who know with greater certainty each day that they have
found the pearl of greatest price: then by the power of the
Cross, O Christ, claim your victory in their heart, and lead
them to the liberty of being seen by all men to be yours, for
your dear name's sake.   Amen.
Dick Williams

CHILDREN'S PRAYERS

93   Thank you Lord for sending your Son Jesus Christ into the
world so that by coming to know him we might also come to
know you;
Thank you Lord Jesus for going to Jerusalem as a King and
for making people take sides either for you or against;
Thank you for showing us how great a difference there is
between serving you and not serving you by being willing
to go to the cross;
Thank you for dying there to save us.
Heavenly Father, help us this week to remember that even
when men were plotting to take his life Jesus spent his time in
loving and serving other people.
Help us this week to love and serve him more, for his dear
sake.   Amen.
Dick Williams

94   We thank you, Lord God, for the goodness of Jesus: we open
our hearts to him so that he may dwell within us and make
us good.
We thank you, Lord God, for the courage of Jesus: help us
like him to stand up for what is right and true.
We thank you, Lord God, for the first disciples who learned
to love Jesus, and who taught others to love him too: help us,
like them, to spread the knowledge of his love.
Help us during this Holy Week to think carefully about
what Jesus did on the last days before his crucifixion.
Help us to understand what happened, and why it happened.
Prepare us to understand more about why Jesus died, and help
us to know that he died for each one of us.
Help us to see more clearly the power of his resurrection and
to share in it by giving our lives to him, for his dear name's
sake.   Amen.
Dick Williams

95   Jesus Christ, when you were born the stable was cold and
dirty; during your life you suffered rejection from those who
ought to have known better; on Good Friday it was grim and
dark. And all this was for me. Thank you, Lord.   Amen.
R. C. Thorp

96   Heavenly Father, we thank you for giving your Son to die on
the cross that we might be forgiven. Help us to understand
the extent of our sin and the greatness of his love, so that we
may trust him as our Saviour and serve him as our Lord.
Amen.
M. H. Botting's collection

97   Heavenly Father there are many roads by which men seek for
truth, and their hearts are only at rest when they find you.
The road to life is the one that leads to a Cross. Help us to
lose our life in this world so that we may find it in you, and
accept your offer of company along the way, through Jesus
Christ our Lord.   Amen.
Joyce Francis

GOOD FRIDAY

98   The Seven Words from the Cross

'Father forgive them for they know not what they do.'
Let us pray for all those who are doing evil. Let us pray for
all proud, violent, and malicious men; let us pray for
blasphemers, unbelievers, heretics; let us pray for all who
exploit their fellow-men, tyrannize them, use them as pawns
in political power struggles; let us pray for all who abuse
power, and so betray the trust placed in them; let us pray for
all who persecute Christians for their faith; let us pray for the
Church when it is tempted to put expediency before truth,
self interest before love, and for the sake of winning human
praise crucifies the Lord afresh; let us pray for ourselves when
lack of zeal, the deceitfulness of riches, and the cares of this
world make us the sleeping partners of social evil.
'Father forgive us, for we know not what we do.'

'This day you shall be with me in paradise.'
Let us pray for all those who want to repent and begin a new
life, but who feel that it is too late; let us pray that they may
learn from the dying thief that Christ is the one nearest to
them, and that paradise is as close as he is. And let us, as one
with the thief, pray as he did: 'Lord remember me'. So may
our last hour blend into the light of paradise, through the
power of the crucified.

'I thirst.'
Let us pray for all who suffer physical distress through lack
of food and water, and for those whose bodies are not able to
benefit from the abundance of food near at hand. Let us pray
that in their hearts they may find rivers of living water to
refresh and sustain them, and prepare the way for physical
relief and healing. And let us pray for all who hunger and
thirst after righteousness; that in their obedience to Christ
they might have meat to eat unknown to them before and,
according to Christ's promise, be satisfied.

'Mother, there is your son. Son, there is your mother.'
Let us pray for family ties. Let us pray for the bereaved; let
us pray that Christ may create relationships which survive the

worst blows which life can give. And let us thank him for his power in creating new relationships which sustain us in the different stages of our pilgrimage.

'My God, my God, why have you forsaken me?'
Let us pray for all who are forsaken; for nations which are forsaken; for children who are forsaken; for old people who are forsaken; for prisoners and captives who are forsaken; for prophets and idealists who are forsaken; and for ourselves when we feel ourselves to be forsaken. May we and all men everywhere find within God's absolute demand his ultimate succour, and understand that below the level of the deepest sorrows are the everlasting arms of his healing love. May we learn to say 'I shall yet give thanks unto him who is my Saviour, my King and my God'.

'It is finished.'
Let us thank Christ for finishing the work that he came to do; let us thank him for having done for us all that is necessary for our salvation; let us thank him that because his work is finished our search for forgiveness is finished and our striving for pardon is finished. And let us thank God that with the end of our search there is the beginning of a life of thankfulness, praise and service, offered to God not from fear but out of love. And let us pray that we may find the work he has for us to do, and finish it.

'Into your hands I commit my spirit.'
Let us thank God that when the conscious control of our life is beyond our grasp we may still repose upon God's eternal changelessness. Teach us, O Lord, to fear the grave as little as we fear our bed; and fill our lives with the hope and faith of the resurrection, in the knowledge that in death our lives pass into the hands which made the world, and guide the universe, the hands of the almighty creator. And may we place our lives in those hands while life is strong and full and sweet, Father, with thanksgiving, into your hands we commit our spirit.
Dick Williams

99   A Children's Prayer

Jesus said, 'There is no greater love than this, that a man
should lay down his life for his friends' (John 15.13).
Let us thank God for sending his Son Jesus into our world.
Let us think of Jesus and pray that we may be more like him.
As we remember his *kindness* in healing and helping,
We know that we should be kind.
  Lord make us more like Jesus.
As we remember his *courage* in facing his enemies,
We know that we should be brave.
  Lord make us more like Jesus.
As we remember how he *forgave* those who put him to death,
We know that we should be forgiving.
  Lord make us more like Jesus.
As we remember his *love* in laying down his life,
We know that we should be loving.
  Lord make us more like Jesus.
Lord God, we are sorry that Jesus was killed. But we thank
you that in this way you have shown how much you love us.
Although we think of his suffering today, we are also glad to
remember that he conquered death and came back alive to be
with his disciples and with us for ever.   Amen.
J. D. Searle

100   Good Friday Evening

Lord, it is hard to concentrate our thoughts for very long on
what happened nearly two thousand years ago. Somehow
the cross on the hill seems so remote from the fireside we
have left and to which we shall return. Yet the sins of those
who crucified Jesus are our sins. Our needs are the needs of
all mankind. Help us tonight to see the cross, eternal not only
in the heart of God but in the hearts of us men and women.
So may we receive your forgiveness and your peace, through
Jesus Christ our Lord.   Amen.
J. D. Searle

EASTER

101 Living God, the resurrection of Jesus throws wide the door between ourselves and life eternal. We go through that door today, inheriting from Christ the ambition to serve you totally, and to spread your kingdom.
Give us, we pray, the power to turn thought into action, and ambition into achievement, through Jesus Christ our Lord. Amen.
Dick Williams

102 O Christ, who lived to show what life is like, who died to show that sin is death, who rose to raise us up to life eternal, help us to follow you and love you, forever. Amen.
Dick Williams

103 Father, we thank you that in finding you we also find new friends and the happiness of much love. When we have entered into this fellowship help us to give ourselves to it, and welcome others into it, through Jesus Christ our Lord. Amen.
Dick Williams

104 O God, whose will is our peace, help us to want for ourselves the things you want us to have; help us to love your programme for living; help us to welcome your orders for the day; for when these prayers are answered our heart will find its home; through Jesus Christ our Lord. Amen.
Dick Williams

105 Loving Father, help us to abandon that love of self which leads to death, and enable us to cause that kind of self-esteem itself to die; help us to be willing for all to be lost except love for you; help us to die to self: then, Lord, help us to live to Christ, and grant us the power of the life he came to bring. For his name's sake. Amen.
Dick Williams

106 Lord Jesus, our risen Saviour, we rejoice in your mighty
victory over sin and death. You are the prince of life; you are
alive for evermore. Help us to know your presence, not only
as we worship you here, but at home, and at work, and
wherever we go; for your great name's sake. Amen.
M. H. Botting's collection

107 **Easter Mission**

Lord Jesus set our hearts on fire with your love that with
joy and thankfulness in our hearts we, your followers, may
once again set out inspired by the message of the Cross and
the joy of Easter Day. Amen.
Joyce Francis

108 What are we for, Creator infinite, if not to show your
likeness to men? May we not hide you by our ways, nor stand
between our neighbour and the truth. So may all men know
that for their present sin you atoned, and that you do not live
only within the past. So may all hungry hearts find purpose
and find life in you, O bringer back from death; and then
salute the Saviour till he comes. Amen.
based on a prayer by Alan Godson

109 **The Road to Emmaus**

Luke 24.13
Lord, we do not always find it easy to recognize your
coming to us. Often our spirits are downcast and we, who
looked for so much in Christ, are frankly disappointed. Will
you reveal yourself to us. Open our eyes to undiscovered
secrets of your Word. Meet us in the breaking of bread. Set
our heavy hearts on fire with love for you and send us on
our way rejoicing. For your name's sake. Amen.
Ian D. Bunting

110 **To Simon**

Luke 24.34
What have we done to deserve your appearing? Like Simon
we have denied you in the inmost secret of our hearts. We

have denied you with our lips, and yet you have marked our
tears and read our thoughts. We thank you for that love
which always comes to us. Help us never to forget your mercy
and keep us, like Simon, faithful to the end.   Amen.
Ian D. Bunting

111   Through Tears

John 20.11
We cannot see for tears. We cannot even recognize the gentle
voice of Jesus; 'Why are you weeping?' Help us in our
sorrows to know that he is near, to feel that he cares and even
to rejoice in his risen power. In faith may we meet him for he
is our Lord, and we love him, Jesus Christ our Saviour.   Amen.
Ian D. Bunting

112   The Grave

Matthew 28.1
O Lord, we miss our loved ones so much that we want to be
near them. Yet you have risen from the grave and assured us
of their happiness. Forgive us the lack of faith which takes
our memory back to the sad day of parting. Lift our eyes to
that day when we shall meet again in Jesus Christ our
Lord.   Amen.
Ian D. Bunting

113   Peace be with You

John 20.19
As Christians, we have no right to fear and yet we are afraid:
of the neighbours, of the people we work with, and even of
our own families. Frequently our faith is found behind the
locked doors of our hearts. And yet, O Lord, you come to us
with peace and the coming is enough to fill our hearts with
joy. Burst the bars of fear that keep us silent and send us on
your errands, your message not only in our hearts but on our
lips. For your name's sake.   Amen.
Ian D. Bunting

114 Thomas

John 20.26
Our Lord and God, forgive the doubting heart in each of us,
which questions your resurrection. We are men of our age
and want to see and touch before we believe. And yet we thank
you for that blessing, reserved for those who do not see and
yet believe. Grant us that faith which looks to Jesus, risen
from the dead, our Saviour and our living Lord. Amen.
Ian D. Bunting

115 Make a Catch

John 21.4
Sometimes, Lord, you seem to us as a stranger on the shore.
Then you remind us of our calling. You challenge us with
hard commandments. You draw out our trust. And then,
when we obey you, you reveal yourself – not as a stranger
but as a friend! Help us to discover you again today, as we do
what you tell us. For your name's sake. Amen.
Ian D. Bunting

116 Witnesses

Acts 1.8
We thank you, Lord Jesus, for your last words. We treasure
them for the promise of your Holy Spirit to give us power.
Help us now to obey your command to be witnesses to the
ends of the earth; starting from where we are now. In your
name we pray. Amen.
Ian D. Bunting

117 The Great Commission

Matthew 28.18
Lord Jesus Christ, to whom is given full authority in heaven
and on earth, give us such a sense of your power that we may
obey your will. Make us disciples in all nations. Make us
messengers to all people. And we thank you that your presence
will be with us this day wherever we go in your name. Amen.
Ian D. Bunting

118   With Great Joy

Luke 24.53
We thank you, Lord, that you did not leave us without your
blessing. You have put a new song on our lips and a new joy
in our hearts. We praise you for a risen Saviour. We rejoice
in a living Lord: and offer our lives today in thankful sacrifice
to Jesus Christ our Lord.   Amen.
Ian D. Bunting

119   To Me Also

1 Corinthians 15.8
We thank you, Father, for every Christian who bears witness
to the risen power of Jesus Christ. We have not seen as the
apostles have seen, but we have met him in our lives; and we
shall never be the same again. That meeting has changed us.
As faithful ambassadors, may we be able to introduce others
to him, that they too may meet our Lord and Saviour Jesus
Christ.   Amen.
Ian D. Bunting

120   A Litany of the Resurrection

We confess, O Lord, that death is the great enemy in our
lives. So strong that it is hard to believe that Jesus is not
buried in Palestine.
The angel said 'He is not here'
     'He has been raised again'.
We envy those who saw him face to face and feel for Thomas
in his doubt. And yet we know he lives.
Jesus said 'Happy are they who never saw me'
     'And yet have found faith'.
In the world we know we should be bold in the Master's
service but we find ourselves fearful and ill equipped.
Jesus said 'You will receive power'
     'When the Holy Spirit comes upon you'.
We would prefer to be quiet Christians. The responsibility of
making Jesus known is a heavy one.

Jesus said 'You shall bear witness for me'
  'To the ends of the earth'.
We are disciples of the Lord. We commit ourselves to his
service and in his risen power resolve to make him known;
by the way we live and by the words we speak. For
overwhelming victory is ours through him who loved us,
even Jesus Christ our Saviour.   Amen.
Ian D. Bunting

121   Homemaker's Prayer After Easter

The Easter eggs have been eaten, Lord; the holiday is nearly
over. Soon the children will be back at school. And what
remains of our glad Easter worship?
The memory of an empty cross? The bare fact that you
conquered death? No, for at the root of life, and interwoven in
its suffering and dying, loving and creating, there is bread.
And Jesus took this, and blessed, and broke it, and said
'This is my body, which is given for you. Do this in
remembrance of me.' We thank you for your body, our bread,
freely offered to release us from the power of sin. We thank
you for this simple sign to remember you by. May the breaking
of bread give us strength in our bodies and in our hearts
each day to do your will, until you return in your glory.
Amen.
Patricia Mitchell

122   Thanksgiving for Resurrection Power

Risen Lord, we thank you for the varied and vivid accounts
given to us by those who actually talked with you and ate
with you and touched you. We thank you for this visible,
physical evidence of your power over death. And we thank
you, too, for the invisible spiritual evidence which each of us
can experience in his heart, which declares to us that Jesus
Christ is still alive. May we, like the first disciples, be brave
enough to tell what we have seen and heard so that everyone
may enjoy the friendship which we have with you and which
is our greatest blessing; for your dear name's sake.   Amen.
Patricia Mitchell

123   Resurrection Joy

Heavenly Father, we thank you for all your goodness to us,
and especially at this time when we rejoice in the knowledge
of Christ's victory over death. Help us to understand and
appreciate more deeply all that the resurrection means and
may we show in our lives the joy which belief in Christ's
promise brings, and so draw others into the experience of your
love and its power to change lives; for his dear name's sake.
Amen.
Patricia Mitchell

124   Faith

Almighty God, our Father, we have seen you in the evidence
of changed lives and in the growth of the Church from
eleven men in Jerusalem to a world-wide fellowship which
has spread through time and space: but sometimes we still
doubt.
We have seen present day missionaries leave all to follow you:
but sometimes we still doubt.
We have seen famous sceptics changed into compassionate,
caring Christians: but sometimes we still doubt.
We have seen the burning joy of men and women who have
undergone great torture and persecution for their faith: but
sometimes we still doubt.
Father, each time we doubt use this experience to build up
our faith. You do not offer us a blind faith but one we can
prove through the help of your Holy Spirit. May we persevere
in looking for answers in the right places and from the right
people; through Jesus Christ our Lord.   Amen.
Patricia Mitchell

CHILDREN'S PRAYERS FOR EASTER
125   A Prayer of Praise

O God, our Father, we thank you for this happy day. Thank
you for Easter eggs and cards and for being on holiday. We
thank you because these things remind us of the true meaning
of Easter.

We remember with gladness:
That Jesus overcame death and showed himself to his friends:
we praise you:
> *We thank you.*

That he is alive for evermore: we praise you:
> *We thank you.*

That he is with us now to be our Friend: we praise you:
> *We thank you.*

That he will always be with us, to the end of time: we praise
you:
> *We thank you.*

Thank you, Lord God, for the good news of Easter.   Amen.
John D. Searle

126   A Prayer of Petition

When we feel sad or worried;
When we are frightened or lonely:
> *Help us to know you are near us.*

When our friends go against us;
When people make us annoyed:
> *Help us to know you are near us.*

When work seems hard or dull;
When we need help to keep us from doing wrong:
> *Help us to know you are near us.*

When everything is going well and
When we are full of happiness:
> *Help us to know you are near us.*

Lord Jesus Christ help us to know that nothing can ever
separate us from your love.   Amen.
John D. Searle

THE ASCENSION

127   Help us, Lord, to understand the meaning of the Ascension.
Help us to accept, in all its wonder, the glorious fact of your
life on earth, and may our vision of it become fuller and
sharper every day; so may we share the blessings of your first
disciples.

Help us to accept your going from the world, and to
understand it not as deprivation but as the pathway to
power unlimited by time and space.
Help us to look for your coming, not in flesh that we see and
touch, but by your dwelling in the brotherhood, and by your
spirit in our mind and heart and soul.
And by the gift of that same spirit, Lord, help us to live a
life on earth which will give to all men everywhere a full,
clear vision of your grace and truth, your beauty and your
reality, here and now, until you come at the end of the ages
as judge and king, O Lord, the same Lord, yesterday, today
and forever.   Amen.
Dick Williams

128   Lord Jesus, we thank you that you ascended as King of
heaven and earth and that you are in control of all things.
Help us to trust you when life is difficult and obey you at all
times. We ask this for the honour of your name.   Amen.
M. H. Botting's collection

129   **Ascensiontide**

Jesus, our teacher and example, in three years you trained the
disciples for their work and then left them with the
uncomfortable power of the Holy Spirit. Help missionaries
and others to learn to be expendable, to know how to teach
and train others, to know when to hand over and move on.
Help them to get out gracefully when their work is done, for
you yourself became expendable for the good of the Church.
Amen.
J. Wheatley Price

PENTECOST

130   Luke 4.18–19
May the spirit of the Lord be upon us that we may announce
good news to the poor, proclaim release for the prisoners,
and recovery of sight for the blind; that we may let the broken
victim go free, and proclaim the year of the Lord's favour;
according to the example of Christ and by his grace.   Amen.

131   Isaiah 11.2

Grant us Lord the spirit of wisdom and insight, the spirit of counsel and power, the spirit of knowledge and of the fear of the Lord; to make us quick in understanding, and true in judgment; according to the example of Christ and by his grace. Amen.

132   Acts 2
Bless us Lord, when we are all together with one consent in one place, and grant that in our common life we may know the coming of your spirit:
Make our hearts as one and clothe our mind with fire; then make us Lord, separately and together, preachers of your good news whom all the world shall hear and understand.
Through Jesus Christ our Lord.   Amen.

133   Galatians 5.22–24

Grant to us Lord the fruit of the spirit: and may your life in ours fulfil itself in love, joy, peace; patience, kindness, goodness; faithfulness, gentleness and self-control. May our lower nature, with its passions and desires, be crucified with Christ, that true life may come. And may the Holy Spirit, the source of that new life, direct its course to your glory, through Jesus Christ our Lord.   Amen.
the above four adaptations of Scripture by Dick Williams

134   We thank you, God our Father, for sending your Holy Spirit
To guide and strengthen us,
To help us understand the Bible and to love and serve the Lord Jesus;
For his sake.   Amen.
Christopher Idle

135   We praise you, O God, because you gave the Holy Spirit to the first Christians. You made Jesus real to them; you taught them the truth and gave them power to witness boldly. Fill us with the same Spirit that we may know their experience and follow their example; for Jesus' sake.   Amen.
M. H. Botting's collection

136   Power to Communicate

When people are all around us, Lord,
And we see their unseeing eyes and know them to be lost in
their private world,
Unable to see a sparrow die:
Lord, help us to communicate.
Break through the barriers of men's minds:
Help us, Lord, to help each other with the gospel of the
risen Lord, that every race be friends; for his name's sake.
Amen.
based on a prayer by Susan Heywood

137   Living Lord, traveller in the way of men, our trail blazer into
eternity, kindle in our hearts the passionate fire of heaven;
burn from our minds the cancer of selfish thought. So may
we dare to imitate your love, and risking all through your
emboldening, dare to share your truth at all times and in all
ways, bringing glory to your name, now and forever.   Amen.
Based on a prayer by Alan Godson

138   A Children's Prayer for Pentecost

(*It may be appropriate to read or outline the story of the Day of
Pentecost as a preface to this prayer.*)

We remember today how the coming of God's Holy Spirit on
the Day of Pentecost changed the lives of the disciples.
Loving Lord God,
Thank you for the joy of the disciples.
We need the gift of joy:
    Give us your Spirit, Lord.
Thank you for the courage of the disciples.
We need the gift of courage:
    Give us your Spirit, Lord.
Thank you for the goodness and unselfishness of the disciples.
We need these gifts:
    Give us your Spirit, Lord.
Thank you for the way the disciples spread the good news of
your love.

We need to be your messengers:
> *Give us your Spirit, Lord.*

Thank you for the disciples' certainty that Jesus would always be with them.
We need his friendship and help:
> *Give us your Spirit, Lord.*

Lord, help us to feel your living Spirit present with us as we worship and at all times.   Amen.

John D. Searle

139   A Responsive Prayer for the Gift of the Holy Spirit

(The results of possessing the Spirit of Jesus are listed by Paul in his letter to the Christians at Galatia (5.22). This verse may be read, possibly by a child, before making the prayer.)

The harvest of the Spirit is love:
Lord Jesus, we know that you taught us to love one another, and yet we sometimes find ourselves hating other people. It is so hard to be loving when others annoy us or are nasty to us. We need a spirit of love.
> *Please give us your Spirit, Lord Jesus.*

The harvest of the Spirit is joy and peace:
Lord Jesus, there are some days when we wake up feeling miserable and all out of sorts. We try to be calm but somehow we feel irritable and quarrelsome.
We need a spirit of joy and peace.
> *Please give us your Spirit, Lord Jesus.*

The harvest of the Spirit is patience and kindness:
Lord Jesus, you know how impatient we can be with each other especially when other people seem slow to understand us. Some days, instead of being kind, we feel we really want to hurt people.
We need a spirit of patience and kindness.
> *Please give your Spirit, Lord Jesus.*

The harvest of the Spirit is goodness and fidelity (faithfulness):
Lord Jesus, sometimes we are in a mood when we want to be good and reliable. At other times we feel we just want to be bad. We cannot understand ourselves for being like this, but

we are glad to know you understand us and still love us.
We need a spirit of goodness and fidelity, (faithfulness).
>   *Please give us your Spirit, Lord Jesus.*

The harvest of the Spirit is gentleness and self-control:
Lord Jesus, it is often lack of thought which causes us to be
rough or even cruel. Strong feelings rise within us and we
find it so hard to be in control of ourselves.
We need a spirit of gentleness and self-control.
>   *Please give us your Spirit, Lord Jesus.*

Amen.
John D. Searle

140   Worship

O God our Father, you seek men and women who will
worship you in spirit and in truth;
And so we ask you to inspire and bless the worship week by
week in this church, in words and music, prayers and hymns,
psalms and lessons.
Open the hearts and lips of those who worship you today all
over the world;
That all of us may listen with an alert conscience to the
preaching of your Word, and come to receive the
Sacrament with true repentance and faith.
We ask this in the name of him, through whom alone our
worship is acceptable to you, our Lord and Saviour, Jesus
Christ.   Amen.
Christopher Idle

TRINITY SUNDAY

141   Almighty God, grant to all Christians everywhere a new
understanding of your kingdom, a new knowledge of your
power, a fresh vision of your glory; and so awaken us to the
reality of your presence that we may be caught up in your
purposes and serve you with a burning spirit and a quiet
mind, through Jesus Christ our Lord.   Amen.
Dick Williams

142   A Children's Prayer

Holy Father God, all the universe belongs to you.
We worship you because you are the Lord of the world, the
stars and space.
We praise you because you have made everything so
wonderfully.
We give you thanks because we know that every good thing
comes from you.
We know that you are all goodness, that you are a holy God.
We are sorry for those times when we fail to be good.
Help us to know you will forgive us and help us to be better.
We come now to worship you in the beauty of holiness.
Amen.
John D. Searle

HARVEST
143   A Thanksgiving

Creator God, we thank you for your promise that while the
earth endures seedtime and harvest, summer and winter, day
and night, shall not fail; we thank you for the reliability of
this good earth; for the variety of the seasons, and all the
contrasts and unity of creation. Thank you for this world's
agenda for the labours of men; for permitting them to enter
into the earth's activity, and to nourish the miracle of their life
upon the miracle of harvest. And so, for the humility of our
dependence upon a marvel we have not manufactured, and for
the dignity of sharing in the work of your almighty hands, we
thank and praise you, God blessed for ever.   Amen.
Dick Williams

144   A Thanksgiving for Beauty in Creation

We thank you, Lord, for the beauty and diversity of the
world which you have made to be the home and mother of
mankind. We thank you for making its hospitality to man endless
in interest, loveliness, diversity and utility. Teach us by your
creation to know more of you our Creator, and rejoicing in
you, to be as generous to others as you are to us;
through Jesus Christ our Lord.   Amen.
Dick Williams

145 Creator God, you have provided man with everything he needs for life and health. Grant that the resources of the earth may not be hoarded by the selfish or squandered by the foolish, but that all may share your gifts, through our Lord Jesus Christ. Amen.
M. H. Botting's collection

146 Thanksgiving

O Lord God, we thank you for all your blessings; for life and health, for laughter and fun; for all powers of mind and body; for our homes and the love of dear ones; for everything that is beautiful, good, and true; but above all for giving us your Son to be our saviour and friend. May we always find our true happiness in pleasing you and helping others to know and love you. Amen.
M. H. Botting's collection

147 Agricultural Workers

Thank you, Lord, for our companions who, through work in field and farm, earn their livelihood by providing us with ours. Give them good working conditions, happy relations with the rest of the community, a fair reward for their labours, and the satisfaction which can come from seeing the works of the Lord in the labour of their hands; through Jesus Christ our Lord. Amen.
Dick Williams

148 Agricultural Research

Eternal Father, whose mind devised the mightiness of seeds, and measured the marvels of harvest, bless all those who seek to understand the mysteries of creation. Make their thoughts to be partners of your own, and grant that from the union of divine wisdom and human endeavour men might discover your provision for their needs. So may the resources of creation be increasingly released to meet the needs of mankind; through Jesus Christ our Lord. Amen.
Dick Williams

149   An Awareness of our Humanity

God who made man for a garden and set him to tend the
earth, be near to us and all the millions of people whose life
is far removed from an environment natural to our humanity.
Help us not to forget the sources of our physical life, no matter
how deeply these may be buried beneath the sophistications
of our urban and industrial life. May the world of trade and
commerce never blind us to the simple equation of soil and
toil which gives us bread, through Jesus Christ our Lord.
Amen.
Dick Williams

150   True Enjoyment

Lord Jesus Christ, who came to earth that we might have
life, and that we might have it abundantly; give us the capacity
always to enjoy your gifts to us, and especially the gift of life
itself; that through these gifts we may learn to enjoy the
supreme gift of eternal life, shared forever with you and the
Father and the Holy Spirit, world without end.   Amen.
Andrew Warner

151   Responsible Enjoyment

God, our Father, we thank you for the world, and for all your
gifts to us, for the sky above, the earth beneath our feet,
and the wonderful process which provides food to maintain
life. We thank you for our crops, and for the skills and
techniques needed to grow and use them properly. Help us to
use your gifts in the spirit of the giver, through Jesus Christ
our Lord.   Amen.

J. R. Worsdall

152   We thank you, God, for the harvest of all good things; for
making plants to grow in the earth; for giving men strength
to work; for supplying the food we have each day. Teach us
to use your gifts fairly and generously and to remember that
you gave them to us; in the name of Jesus Christ.   Amen.
Christopher Idle

153 A Countryman's Litany at Harvest

Surrounded by the beauty of these flowers, let us thank God for the beauty of his creation; let us thank him for all the joy and wonder that comes to us through the appreciation of beauty and colour. And let us pray for those who are blind or whose sight is fading.
Lord, in thy mercy:
Hear our prayer.

All the flowers, fruit and vegetables here were grown in our gardens, but thousands of people have no gardens where they can grow things and have few open spaces where their children can play. Let us pray for children who have never picked a flower from their own garden and for youngsters who have never climbed a tree. Let us pray too for parents facing each day the frustrations of living in tall blocks of flats or in filthy slums.
Lord, in thy mercy:
Hear our prayer.

The things which have been brought to this church are part of our plenty but millions never have enough to eat. Let us ask God's forgiveness for our indifference to the needs of others. Let us ask God's forgiveness that we forget that much of the wealth of this country was gained by exploiting others. Let us pray that as a nation and as individuals we may take seriously our responsibilities for those who are starving.
Lord, in thy mercy:
Hear our prayer.

Today we thank God for the provision of our needs as individuals, but God is also concerned for us as a community. Let us pray for our community life here; let us pray for those in positions of leadership and authority here; let us pray for those who have recently moved here; and let us pray for those who find it difficult to accept the changes taking place.
Lord, in thy mercy:
Hear our prayer.

The beauty of the flowers and the provision of our physical needs cause us to think of God, but millions in our land and

overseas do not know of God's love for them and have never
responded to Christ's invitation 'Come unto me and I will
give you rest.' Let us pray for those who have never trusted
their lives to Christ. Let us pray for ourselves and our
representatives in the Missionary Societies as together we tell
people of the Lord Jesus Christ and his love for them.
Lord in thy mercy:

> *Hear our prayer.*

Today we have remembered to thank God for his goodness
to us, but this reminds us that often we forget to thank him,
and we just take God and his love for granted. Let us ask for
his forgiveness and pray that we may never be complacent
about the good things which we enjoy.
Lord, in thy mercy:

> *Hear our prayer.*
>
> Peter Markby

154   Children's Prayer at Harvest Thanksgiving

As we see the gifts brought here to remind us of God's
kindness, let us give him our thanks for the food we eat.
For food which grows in gardens –
lettuces, beans, carrots and tomatoes: for these gifts,

> *We thank you, God our Father.*

For fields of peas, potatoes, cabbages and sugar beet: for these
gifts,

> *We thank you, God our Father.*

For crops of wheat and the flour for making bread and cakes:
for these gifts,

> *We thank you, God our Father.*

For apples and pears and plums grown in orchards: for these
gifts,

> *We thank you, God our Father.*

For the harvest of the sea –
fish and crabs and shrimps: for these gifts,

> *We thank you, God our Father.*

For food from other lands –
Bananas and oranges and fruit in tins: for these gifts,

> *We thank you, God our Father.*

For the work of farmers, fishermen, shopkeepers and all who
provide the things we need: for these gifts,
   We thank you, God our Father.
We thank you, God our Father, for your love in giving so
much to us. Help us to remember that your gifts are meant
for everyone. Help us to find ways of sharing with those who
are poor or hungry. For your love's sake.   Amen.
John D. Searle

155   Prayers for Animals

God, who has given us animals to share with us our life on
earth, help us to show our gratitude to you by treating our
livestock humanely, and grant that men may give the animals
in their charge happy and contented lives, in return for the
food and service which they provide for us. We ask this
through Jesus Christ our Lord.   Amen.
J. R. Worsdall

156   We pray for farm animals, especially those living lives
distorted by suffering in order to satisfy human greed. Grant
that the human race may realize that animals are our fellow
creatures, and that God is concerned about them too; through
Jesus Christ our Lord.   Amen.
J. R. Worsdall

157   O Lord God, who at creation gave man dominion over the
animals, and to whom we must one day answer for our
stewardship, inspire us with true reverence for your creation.
Guide into the way of kindness all who have the care of
animals, and bless all who work to relieve or prevent suffering
among them. We ask this in the name of Jesus Christ our
Lord.   Amen.
Andrew Warner

158   Father in heaven, whose tender mercies are over all your work,
send your blessing on those who minister to sick and
suffering animals and hasten the day when the whole of the
animal creation shall be delivered from the bondage of
cruelty and fear; through Jesus Christ our Lord.   Amen.
F. O. Owens

159   Blessed Lord, Father of compassion, you hate nothing you
have made, but love all things great and small, and you mark
the sparrow's fall; by your gracious care foxes have holes and
the birds of the air have nests: bless all your creatures
abundantly. Feed them; shelter them from wind and
weather; shield them from terror and torment. Heal their
wounds and alleviate their griefs and pains; for the sake of
him who loved them, Jesus Christ our Lord.   Amen.
Douglas Pegler

160   Lord, teach us to accept with gratitude and delight the beauty
and wonder of the animal creation. You made them, they are
yours, and you have given them into our hands. Through
greed, through selfishness, even through curiosity we
woefully misuse them. Change the hearts of all men so that
these things shall not be. Teach us to understand that there is
a price of suffering too high to pay so that we may a little
prolong our lives. We dare not ask pardon for all the cruelties
of laboratory, of modern farming, and so many other things;
only we pray that, through Jesus Christ, we may become
merciful to the helpless.   Amen.
Doris Rybot

161   Stewardship

You are rich, O God, in mercy, grace and love; grant your
pity on all who are rich in other ways; those with too much
money, too much food, too many possessions, and hearts that
prefer these things to yourself.
Guard us from the love of earthly things; teach us the blessings
of being generous, and the honour of being stewards of what
belongs to you. And to all who are trapped by the snare of
money, grant a sight of the compelling attractiveness of the
wealth of Christ, who though he was rich yet for our sakes
became poor.
We pray this in his name.   Amen.
Christopher Idle

162   Industry and Work

Almighty God, you give men wisdom to think, and skill to
complete all kinds of work. Help all who labour with hand
and brain, that seeking the best in their job they may find joy
in their work; through Jesus Christ our Lord.   Amen.
M. H. Botting's collection

MEMORIAL DAYS

163   Father, Forgive
'All have sinned and come short of the glory of God'
(Romans 3.23).

The hatred which divides nation from nation, race from race,
class from class,
>   *Father, forgive.*

The covetous desires of men and nations to possess what is
not their own,
>   *Father, forgive.*

The greed which exploits the labours of men, and lays waste
the earth,
>   *Father, forgive.*

Our envy of the welfare and happiness of others,
>   *Father, forgive.*

Our indifference to the plight of the homeless and the refugee,
>   *Father, forgive.*

The lust which uses for ignoble ends the bodies of men and
women,
>   *Father, forgive.*

The pride which leads us to trust in ourselves, and not in God,
>   *Father, forgive.*

Be kind one to another, tenderhearted, forgiving one another
as God in Christ forgave you.[1]

J. W. Poole
© the Provost and Chapter of Coventry Cathedral.
Reproduced by permission
[1] Ephesians 4.32.

164 An Act of Resolve

It is our resolve to save succeeding generations from the
scourge of war, which twice in this century has brought
untold sorrow to mankind.
Lord help us.
It is our resolve to reaffirm our faith in fundamental human
rights, in the dignity and worth of the human person, in the
equal rights of men and women and of nations large and small.
Lord help us.
It is our resolve to establish conditions under which justice
and respect for the obligations arising from treaties and other
sources of international law can be maintained, and to promote
social progress and better standards of life in larger freedom.
Lord help us.
And for these ends it is our resolve to practise tolerance and
live together in peace with one another as good neighbours.
Lord help us.
It is our resolve to unite our strength to maintain
international peace and security, and to ensure that armed
force shall not be used, save in the common interest.
Lord help us.
It is our resolve to employ international machinery for the
promotion of the economic and social advancement of all
peoples.
Lord help us.
Amen.
Liverpool Cathedral
based on the preamble to the United Nations Charter

165 An Act of Remembrance

Father, you do not need us to bring before you the needs of
war-sufferers: you know all about them. Your compassion is
the same, whether we remember them or not. It is we who
need to remember. We remember them before you now. We
remember them because you are their father as well as ours.
(*Silence*)
We thank you Father for reminding us that remembrance is
not enough; for reminding us that helping them is the Christian

family's business. We remember them so that you may guide
us into the best way of helping them.
(*Silence*)
Save us, Father, from the blasphemy of making intercession
merely an act of church routine. May formal worship not
become meaningless worship. Show us what we must do.
Help us to do it.
(*Silence*)
Let us not plead poverty of time, or money, or talent, for
we can always find time to do what we want to do: we can
always find money to spend on what we really desire: we can
always find jobs within our powers. Help us to help the
helpless. Turn our prayer into action. And give our action
good success; through Jesus Christ our Lord.   Amen.
L. Watson (adapted)

166   **Those Who Suffer Because of War**

O Saviour Christ, in whom there is neither Jew nor Greek,
East nor West, black nor white, we pray for all, of
whatever nation, who suffer because of human strife; especially
for those least able to receive human help; those whose
hearts are still bitter; those whom we remember today.
We pray that through your ministry of love and life, their
wounds of body and spirit may be healed, and that in you
men may find peace with God and peace with one another;
for your truth and mercy's sake.   Amen.
Christopher Idle

167   O Father of mercies and God of all comfort, whose Son
ministered to those in need; remember for good all who
suffer through the wars of men and nations, by loss of home or
faculties, by loss of friends and loved ones, by loss of
happiness or security or freedom.
Look upon our world, still torn apart by violence and
fighting, and grant success to those who work for peace:
through him who reconciled men with God, and men with
men, the Lord Jesus Christ.   Amen.
Christopher Idle

168   **Soldiers**

Father, we pray for all young soldiers caught up in the
conflict and horror of war. May fear and confusion not lead
them to cruelty. May they show compassion wherever
possible. Enable them to fulfil their duty dispassionately that
their souls may not be scarred by the passions let loose in
war. And we pray for a great outpouring of your Holy
Spirit on all leaders who are responsible for war, that they may
find peaceful ways of solving their countries' problems,
through Jesus Christ our Lord.   Amen.
Patricia Mitchell

169   **Peace**

O living God, your Son Jesus Christ lived and worked in this
world; he knew its hatred and its war, its diseases and its sin.
Please help those who have to find a way out of the
deadlock to progress; a way out of division to harmony; a
way out of selfishness to cooperation; a way out of death to
life.
Grant them wisdom, restraint, and a desire for fair and just
dealing.
Channel the strong desire for peace among many people into
useful and constructive ways of peacemaking;
And bring your own rule of peace among the men you have
created;
For the sake of Jesus Christ your Son.
Christopher Idle

170   O God of power and love, look in mercy upon our war-torn
world, which is still your world;
You have made it; in it you delight to work; you have
redeemed its people.
Grant reconciliation, we ask, between man and man, nation
and nation, through the power of that great peace made by
Jesus your Son;
May your servants not be troubled by wars and rumours of
wars, but rather look up because their redemption draws near;
And when our King returns, may he find many waiting for

him, and fighting with his weapons alone;
We ask this in the King's name, Jesus Christ your Son our
Lord. Amen.
Christopher Idle

171   Peace Through the Gospel

We continue to pray O Lord for the peace of the world. Help
us to see that there can be no peace among nations unless
there is peace among men, and no peace among men until
men have made their peace with you.
We claim the peace which comes from faith in Jesus Christ,
that having peace in our hearts we may be at peace with our
neighbours, and that peace between man and man may finally
grow into peace between nation and nation. We ask this in
the name of the Prince of Peace, our Lord Jesus Christ.
Amen.
Simon H. Baynes

172   Peace
O God we pray that wars may come to an end, and that
domination of one country over another, one class over
another, one colour over another may soon become a thing
of the past; through Jesus Christ our Lord.   Amen.
J. R. Worsdall

173   Peace on Earth

O God, whose being is life and whose ways are peace, we
confess to you with sorrow that wars and strife are all of
mankind's making. Forgive the blasphemy which lays the
blame on you. And give us grace to see that when we blame
ourselves there is a light in our darkness. Then, O God, give
us strength to order our affairs in the power of that light, and
so to love and speak the truth in love that others may look
with us to you and in you find the way, the truth and the life
for all mankind, through Jesus Christ our Lord.   Amen.
Dick Williams

174 Strained International Relations

O God, who made all men of one blood, calling us to be your
sons and so to become brothers in deed and in truth: look in
mercy on the nations which now confront each other in
anger, fear and pride. Enable their leaders to see in their true
perspective those things which divide them, and to see in
their true importance those things which may unite. And in
your grace and mercy, Lord, inspire all men everywhere to
cease from war, and to fight instead for those things which
you have shown us to be right, in Jesus Christ – his life, his
death, his resurrection and his endless life; for his name's
sake.   Amen.
Dick Williams

175 Warmongers

O God, who knows the hearts of men, have mercy on all
those who seek to solve their nation's problems by force of
arms; those who seek to heal their nation's own economy by
promoting international strife; those who divert a nation's
mind from corruption at home by talk of enmity abroad;
those who see young men-at-arms as pawns upon a gaming
board; and all who are eager, through warfare, to barter with
others in flesh and blood. Upon these and all who hate their
brother, have mercy Lord we pray, through Jesus Christ our
Lord.   Amen.
Dick Williams

176 War Correspondents

We thank you, Lord, for the cameramen and journalists who
risk their lives to rob warfare of its glamour. May we take to
heart their portrait of men's pain and never think of war
except in terms of sorrow; through Jesus Christ our Lord.
Amen.
Dick Williams

177   Racial Harmony

O Lord Jesus Christ, Prince of Peace, break down the
barriers which separate men from each other and from God.
Teach Christians to love each other across the walls of colour,
class and creed: forgive us, too, the excuses we make for our
own prejudice. And lead us captive in your cause of peace on
earth, goodwill to men. For your Name's sake.   Amen.
Ian D. Bunting

ALL SAINTS' DAY

178   O Eternal God, help us always to remember the great unseen
cloud of those witnesses who are round about us. When in
danger give us their courage, and when in difficulty, their
perseverance; so that we too may be faithful until we rejoice
with all the saints in your eternal kingdom; through Jesus
Christ our Lord.   Amen.
W. A. Hampson

179   We thank you, O God, for the example of the saints. Help us
to follow in their footsteps with courage and hope, so that
your work on earth may be faithfully continued and your
holy name be praised until the end of the world, through
Jesus Christ our Lord.   Amen.
W. A. Hampson

180   Almighty and everlasting God, we praise your holy name for
all the saints throughout the ages who have kept the lamp of
faith burning brightly. Grant that we who are following in
their steps may keep that light shining, that the darkness of
this world may be lit by him who is the light of the world,
even your Son our Saviour Jesus Christ.   Amen.
W. A. Hampson

Prayers for the World

RULERS AND GOVERNORS

181 The President

Grant, O Lord, to our President simple faith to walk in the
way set before him; patience and courage to bear the burden
laid upon him; humility to know that his authority is but
lent by you; and the sure hope of life with you for ever, to
whom belongs all dignity and greatness, all majesty and
power, in both this world and that which is to come.
Amen.
Simon H. Baynes

182 The President and Those in Authority

Lord God almighty, King of Creation, bless our president and
all in authority under him: may godliness be their guidance;
may sanctity be their strength; may peace on earth be the
fruit of their labours; and joy in heaven their eternal gift,
through Jesus Christ our Lord. Amen.
Dick Williams

183 Almighty God, our heavenly Father, we pray for our President
and his cabinet, the members of Congress, and all in
authority: that they may govern our country with wisdom
and understanding, and for the good of your Church and
people, through Jesus Christ our Lord. Amen.
M. H. Botting's collection

184 Leaders

Grant, O Lord, to all the leaders of men the wisdom to seek
what is right, and the goodness to do it; may learning,
education, and politics all be directed to good ends, and may

godliness among men lead to peace among nations; through
Jesus Christ our Lord.   Amen.
Dick Williams

185   The Nation

Father in Heaven, whose will it is that all men should worship
you in the fellowship of the Church, and serve you in the
life of the world; send down upon our nation a true spirit of
repentance for the sinfulness which passes for broadmindedness,
the apathy which calls itself tolerance, the materialism which
glories in its prosperity and grasps for more. And with this
sorrow, O Lord God, let faith and obedience go hand in
hand, that men's lives may be transformed, that integrity and
godliness may characterize our people, to your praise and
honour; through Jesus Christ our Lord.   Amen.
Michael Saward

186

Grant to our nation, O Lord, a knowledge of that which is
good against which to measure that which is doubtful, by
which to shun what is bad, through which to govern its
desires. Help those who form public opinion and fashion public
tastes never to presume that man is wiser and better than his
forebears, nor to be so foolish as to suppose that he can cope
any better than they with the consequences of sin. And raise
up, we pray, a new knowledge of Christ our Lord in the
hearts and minds of all writers, artists and entertainers, for
the sake of Jesus Christ our Lord.   Amen.
Dick Williams

187   The Government of this Country

O mighty God, the source of all goodness, please bless those
who are in positions of power and authority in this country.
Bless the President and his family, all members of his cabinet
and all legislators in Congress. Enrich them with your
grace and fill them with your Holy Spirit, that we may be
governed with wisdom and godliness by Christian men and
women. And watch over those who help form public opinion,
the press and the broadcasting services; that we may be

enabled to exercise our rights as citizens in a manner which
is responsible and in accordance with your will; through
Jesus Christ our Lord.   Amen.

188   Rulers

O God, our Father and Lord, you have taught us that you are
the ruler of all, the power above all powers. We commit into
your hands all the rulers of the earth, all presidents, kings,
ministers and dictators; and we pray, most merciful Lord,
that your will may be done upon earth, that you will raise up
those whom you will raise up, and throw down those whom
you will throw down. And may we all have confidence when
the peace of the world seems in the balance, realizing that you
alone are the creator and destroyer of kingdoms, even to the
end of time; through Jesus Christ our Lord.   Amen.

189   Rulers and People

O royal Master of men, who commands us to love one another,
grant to the rulers and people of our own and every land the
vision to look beyond national boundaries and racial
ambitions, that in love to you and service to each other they
may bring their gifts and their treasures into the common
fellowship of your kingdom and so promote the unity of all
mankind to the glory of God the Father, the Son and the
Holy Spirit.   Amen.
Harold E. Evans

190   Peace Where There is Civil Strife

O Father, who makes men to be of one mind in their
homeland, great God of peace, bless those nations where
there is civil strife, where neighbour rises up against
neighbour, where familar streets become battlefields, and
familiar people become the casualties: change the hearts of
all those who think that their cause is more important than
another man's right to live; change the policies of those on
either side which create, condone or extend the conflict; and
by the power of the Cross help all who sin to repent, and all

who have been sinned against to forgive, that peace may come, through Jesus Christ our Lord.   Amen.
Dick Williams

191   Our Country

Dear God, who has decreed that righteousness alone makes a nation great, we beseech you so to move the hearts and wills of our leaders and people that in righteousness we may be led, and in righteousness may gladly follow; for the honour of your name, through Jesus Christ our Lord.   Amen.
Tom Farrell

192   The Nation and Peace

O God, from whom alone comes love and trust, and in whom alone men and nations can find peace; send into the hearts of all men everywhere the transforming power of your Spirit so that with new heart and purpose we may seek first your service and the service of one another, and in so doing discover the peace which passes understanding, through Jesus Christ our Lord.   Amen.
Harold E. Evans

193   Personal Peace

Grant us, O Lord, that calm strength of your Spirit in which the fret and chafe of life shall have no power to vex or disturb. So may we serve you with unwearying patience, unclouded vision, and unfaltering love, that we may possess the peace which passes understanding and the joy that none can take from us; through Jesus Christ our Lord.   Amen.
Harold E. Evans

THE CHURCH

194 Lord of the Church, enable your people to be the Church:
a redeemed people;
a holy people;
a united people;
a missionary people;
and, in all things, a people gladly submissive to the truth as it comes to us in Jesus, in whose name we pray. Amen.
Michael Saward

195 Thank you, O God, for the courage and faith of all those men and women who, from the time of the apostles, preached the gospel of the living Christ; those who were strong in the face of persecution; those who brought the good news to this land of ours; and for those, who, in recent years, have gone out to teach and to preach in the name of Christ their Lord.
Be with your Church in every land. Strengthen her when she is weak, encourage her when she is failing, give her humility where she is proud, and self-confident; and where, day by day, she is seeking to show others the joy of your kingdom, deepen her faith in her risen Lord.
Help us to realize that we are a part of your great Church universal and that together with all your children we can worship and adore, through Jesus Christ our Lord. Amen.
author unknown (per Michael Saward)

196 Clergy and People of the Church

O Heavenly God, the same yesterday, and today and forever, pour your blessing upon the ministers and laymen of your Church, in this country and in all lands. May we grasp your majesty and might; may we be filled with your Holy Spirit, that the Church today, like the early Church, may preach and live the gospel of Christ in eagerness, power and love. Grant this, O Lord, that your name may be honoured before the world. Amen.

197   The Life of the Church

O merciful and heavenly God, we commit to you all those
who make up your Church in all the world. Teach us, whom
you have justified, to live by faith; bear us, by your grace,
through all troubles; and bring us at last to the glory of your
eternal kingdom; for the honour of our Saviour and
mediator, Jesus Christ.   Amen.

198   A Prayer of Penitence for the Church

We are ashamed, O God, for our carelessness in worship, for
wandering mind and thoughtless prayer. We are ashamed that
words of praise come so swiftly to our lips but so slowly to
our hearts. We are ashamed that we hear the name of Jesus
but act as if he were a stranger.
Forgive us for our jealousies in the church, and for the
irritations which so easily win the day. Forgive us for the
times when we can see plainly what needs to be done, and
complain that others do not do it.
Give us, O Lord, a vision of our church set as it is among
people who do not know Christ as Lord, and give to us a
deepened faith, an understanding love, a ready wit and the
Holy Spirit's uncommon sense. So may we live, and so preach,
that our neighbours may want to know the source of the joy
we shall have, through Jesus Christ our Lord.   Amen.
author unknown (adapted by Michael Saward)

199   The Church in Time of Change

Guide and direct, O Lord, the minds of all who work for the
reshaping of our church. Restore our faith and vision. Renew
our energies and love. Revive your people to new life and
power. So may we live and speak for Christ before the world
he came to save; for his name's sake.   Amen.
Timothy Dudley-Smith

200   For Congress

Almighty God, direct the hearts and minds of those who bear
in their hands the government of this people. Make them to
uphold honour and justice, to restrain evil and oppression, and
to seek the true prosperity of our country and the welfare of
mankind. Through Jesus Christ our Lord.   Amen.
Timothy Dudley-Smith

201   Our Own Church

Grant, O Lord, a right balance of your powers in us, that in
loving you singly we may not neglect the needs of man, and
that in serving mankind wholeheartedly we may not forget
the joys of the world to come. Give us the gifts of faith and
hope and love in perfect measure; that we may look upwards,
look outwards, and look onwards, with equal eagerness,
through Jesus Christ our Lord.   Amen.
Simon H. Baynes

202   A Parish Awaiting a New Minister

Lord, call to this your church and ours
    a true shepherd
    a servant of God
    a minister of Christ.
Make us a church joyful in worship and united in
    witness,
    working,
    caring,
    praising,
    loving,
to the glory of your Name: through Jesus Christ our Lord.
Amen.
Timothy Dudley-Smith

203   A Thanksgiving for Light in the Church

We thank you Father for your gift of perfect love, Jesus
Christ. We thank you for all who have accepted your gift
and in whom the light shines. For those who seek to improve

the plight of the homeless and badly housed; for the young
people sharing their learning and energy freely through
voluntary service at home and abroad; for all organizations
helping to relieve suffering and distress in stricken lands; for
missionaries living out your message in the midst of
ignorance, fear and disease; for all those who freely give time
and energy and money to bring comfort, hope and help to
someone who needs it. Your light shines in the darkness and
the darkness has not overcome it. We thank you Father for
this, through Jesus Christ our Lord.   Amen.
Patricia Mitchell

204   The World and the Church

We pray, O God, for the nations;
for their right dealing one with another;
for the breaking down of barriers of race and colour;
for political freedom;
for educational development; and for a more just economic
structure.
In the faith that your love is a healing love,
your power a healing power,
your peace a healing peace;
we bring to you the needs of all those who suffer from
disease, hunger, unemployment, loneliness, confusion and fear,
sorrow, depression and guilt.
Enable them to turn to you in faith so that they can receive
the healing which each one needs.
Grant to your Church throughout the world that men may
respond joyously to your love, by committing themselves in
obedience and service, with a faith which is strengthened by a
living experience of Christ's presence, with hearts warmed to
love and with freedom and courage to follow where Christ
leads; for his name's sake.   Amen.
author unknown

205   The Dedication of Churches

O God, who cannot be confined by the vastness of the
universe, nor contained within the infinitude of space:

Almighty Creator, forever present in creation, eternally
present beyond it; have mercy on us who, in fear and
trembling, have built this church (*or who build churches*) for your
praise. Save us from idolatry. As we learn to meet you here,
may we learn to meet you everywhere. And may our reverence
for this place teach us how to view the whole creation;
through Jesus Christ our Lord.   Amen.
Dick Williams

206   Architects

Almighty God, architect of the universe, bless your servants
who design cathedrals, churches and chapels for your praise.
May their work express the majesty of your being, the
integrity of your creation, the pattern of your speech, the
manner of your coming, the nature of your abiding, the spirit
of our response, the shape of our community, the goal of our
discipleship; for your most worthy praise.   Amen.
Dick Williams

UNITY
207   Disunity

Forgive us the sins of disunity, O Lord: pride and
jealousy and narrow mindedness. Forgive us the sins of unity:
lack of imagination, apathy and indifference. Make us one in
genuine love and mutual trust. Make us many in gifts and talents
and vision.   Amen.
Simon H. Baynes

208   Litanies for Unity

Let us thank God that because man is made in his image it is
possible for men to be united. Let us thank him for the
special unity which those who are new creatures in Christ
Jesus can enjoy. Let us ask God to forgive the sin that has
destroyed the unity he meant mankind to have.
Lord in mercy:
Hear our prayer.
Let us thank God for the growth of understanding between

Christians of different outlooks and traditions. Let us thank
him for the growth in unity of our local churches. Let us pray
that we may grow together in truth and love.
Lord in mercy:

Hear our prayer

Let us pray that we may learn from Christians of other
traditions. Let us pray that they may learn from us. May they
and we remember that Jesus prayed for us to be santified in
truth before he prayed for us to be one. Therefore so guide us
that we might seek unity through the truth.
Lord in mercy:

Hear our prayer

Let us pray for our own church, that we and all its members
may be filled with the spirit of faith, hope and love, and so
attain to that unity which will cause people to acknowledge
the truth of our gospel.
Lord in mercy:

Hear our prayer

Let us pray for the community of which we are part. Let us
pray for greater unity between its various sections, interests
and age-groups.
Lord in mercy:

Hear our prayer

Let us pray for the unity of our country, for a greater
understanding and sympathy between the young and those
who are older, between employers and those employed,
between immigrants and the host community, and
between the Church and those who have rejected institutional
Christianity.
Lord in mercy:

Hear our prayer

Finally let us pray for the unity of the world, for reconciliation,
peace and compassion between rich and poor, white and
coloured, capitalist and communist, and those nations which
have long been embattled.
Lord in mercy:

Hear our prayer
Peter Markby (adapted)

209 Let us pray that all God's will for his Church may be fulfilled in it. And on this day let us pray particularly that all ecumenical endeavour might be based firmly upon the Word of God, should have the aim of glorifying the Son of God, should seek the power of the Spirit of God, should bear fruit to the praise of God.

Lord in mercy:

Hear our prayer

Let us pray that in all its present divisions the Church may preach the gospel with growing zeal, growing confidence, growing power; so may the gospel itself unite us. And let us pray that the unity thus given may itself commend and make persuasive the gospel we proclaim.

Lord in mercy:

Hear our prayer

Let us pray that we may be saved from worshipping any tradition, no matter how excellent. Let us pray that we may be saved from worshipping any hope, no matter how glorious. Let us pray that we may be saved from these and all forms of idolatry, that we may be set free to worship God the Father Almighty.

Lord in mercy:

Hear our prayer

Let us pray for all theologians, thinkers and planners who are now engaged in finding the way to outward expressions of unity, that they may deal in godliness and in truth, and exercise their judgment in wisdom and love.

Lord in mercy:

Hear our prayer

Let us pray for all who negotiate any difficult and painful matter which may arise in practical schemes of union, that they may never forget that they are not dealing with institutions, but with people and with the risen Christ.

Lord in mercy:

Hear our prayer

Let us pray for every experiment designed (*like our acts of worship this week*) to help us see the other's tradition through the other's eyes.

Lord in mercy:

Hear our prayer

Let us pray for ourselves in our worship (*tonight*) that our
eyes may not be upon each other, nor upon our differences,
but upon Christ: that we may look to him and be saved.
Lord in mercy:

Hear our prayer

Let us pray for the churches in this parish (*here they may be
mentioned by name*): that each may be blessed by God the Holy
Spirit and be brought to that fullness of life in which we stand
together under the Lordship of Christ.
Lord in mercy:

Hear our prayer

Let us pray for the children of our churches that to them may
be revealed the unfolding purposes of your will and the
vision of the Church as it shall be.
Lord in mercy.

Hear our prayer

And let us pray for ourselves that we may be given a vision
of the world in all its need, and be so inspired by God that
we may serve it with grace and power, and so love the truth,
and live the truth, and speak the truth that all men everywhere
may find the truth, and being set free from sin find the
glorious liberty of the children of God.
Lord in mercy:

Hear our prayer
(*The Grace.*)

210   The Christian Family Tree

'I am the vine, you are the branches. He who dwells in me, as
I dwell in him, bears much fruit.'
Father we thank you for the fact and for the history of our
great family tree, of which we too are branches. And we give
thanks for all those who have brought forth good fruit:
Those who have overcome every hardship in order to take
knowledge of you to all parts of the world.
Those who have dedicated their lives to social work;
Those who have visited prisoners and given them hope.
Those who have fought disease and ignorance;
Those who have brought colour and music and beauty into
our lives through the expression of their faith;

Those who have suffered to keep God's word pure and clear
and free from men's additions;
Those who in their family life have by teaching and example
given to their children the desire to belong to this tree:
Father, we are glad that we too are able to be branches of
this great tree of life and we pray that our lives may bring
forth good fruit, to the glory of your name.   Amen.
Patricia Mitchell

211   Dedication to God's Design

Let us kneel and offer ourselves to God that we may know
how to take our share in his design for the world. Let us pray.
That we may put ourselves alongside our fellow men and see
the Christian faith and life from their point of view:
    Lord, hear our prayer.
That the Church may be aware of the rapid rate of change
both in the thought of men and in their social circumstances:
    Lord, hear our prayer.
For the wisdom of the Holy Spirit in the large-scale and
complex problems of society and work today, which require
corporate judgments and solutions:
    Lord, hear our prayer.
That in the choices facing mankind today in situations partly
good and partly evil, we may be granted the insights of the
Holy Spirit, and guided to make decisions which will forward
your will:
    Lord, hear our prayer.
That you will grant to Christians working in big organizations
the faith that they can share in some small way your active
concern for the good ordering of men's lives and the
supplying of their needs:
    Lord, hear our prayer.
That we may see in our daily work the opportunity for
serving you by the truth of our insights, the honesty of our
service, and the concern for our fellow-workers:
    Lord, hear our prayer.
That you will bless those groups of Christians who are trying
to discover how they may best exercise Christian vocation
through their professions:

Lord, hear our prayer.

That our local churches may no longer be seen as arks of safety, but as power-houses of grace for the invading forces of your Kingdom:

Lord, hear our prayer.

That you will bless and guide all lay movements which seek to advance your Kingdom in special spheres of work or in particular neighbourhoods:

Lord, hear our prayer.

That you will guide our local churches to face the challenge of such movements, to learn from them and to offer understanding and grateful fellowship:

Lord, hear our prayer.

That you will enable the clergy to bring the light of your truth to their people and the grace of the Sacraments to their strengthening:

Lord, hear our prayer.
Liverpool Cathedral

212   Week of Prayer for Christian Unity

We are come together in the presence of Almighty God to offer to him our worship and praise and thanksgiving, to make confession of our sins and to pray for the recovery of the unity of Christ's Church and for the renewal of our common life together, through Jesus Christ in whom we are all made one.

Wherefore let us give heed to the words of Holy Scripture setting forth God's will and purpose for the unity of his Church.

'Hear, O Israel, the Lord our God is one Lord; and you shall love the Lord your God with all your heart, and with all your soul, and with all your mind.'

Lord, write your Word in our hearts.

That we may know and do your will.

'There is one body, and one Spirit, as there is also one hope held out in God's call to you; one Lord, one faith, one baptism; one God and Father of all, who is over all and

through all and in all.'
Lord write your Word in our hearts.
That we may know and do your will.
'For Christ is like a single body with its many limbs and
organs, which, many as they are, together make up one body.
For indeed we were all brought into one body by baptism, in
the one Spirit, whether we are Jews or Greeks, whether
slaves or freemen, and that one Holy Spirit was poured out
for all of us to drink.'
Lord, write your Word in our hearts.
That we may know and do your will.
'But it is not for these alone that I pray, but for those also
who through their words put their faith in me; may they all
be one; as thou, Father, art in me, and I in thee, so also may
they be in us, that the world may believe that thou didst send
me.'
Lord, write your Word in our hearts.
That we may know and do your will.

(*The Act of Penitence*)
Let us ask God's forgiveness for the sins by which we have
hindered the recovery of unity and caused the Christian name
to be blasphemed.
Lord, have mercy upon us.
Christ, have mercy upon us.
For the sins of thought; for ignorance of the faith by which
our fellow Christians live; for intellectual pride and
isolation;
for the rejection of truth which we have never tried to
understand.
Lord, have mercy upon us.
Christ, have mercy upon us.
For the sins of temper; for apathy and complacency, for
prejudice and party spirit; for hasty judgment and embittered
controversy.
Lord, have mercy upon us.
Christ, have mercy upon us.
Pardon, O Lord, we pray you, the sins of our past ignorance
and wilfulness; uplift our hearts in love and energy and

devotion, that being made clean from guilt and shame we may go forward to serve you and your Church in newness of life, through Jesus Christ our Lord.   Amen.

(*The Act of Intercession*)
Blessed be the Kingdom of the Father and of the Son and of the Holy Spirit, now and forever, and into all eternity.
　Amen.
In peace let us pray to the Lord.
　Lord, show your mercy.
For the peace that is from above, and for the salvation of our souls, let us pray to the Lord.
　Lord, show your mercy.
For the peace of the whole world; for the stability of the holy churches of God and for the unity of all, let us pray to the Lord.
　Lord, show your mercy.
For this holy house, and for those who enter it with faith, reverence and the fear of God, let us pray to the Lord.
　Lord, show your mercy.
For this city, and for every city and land, and for the faithful who dwell in them, let us pray to the Lord.
　Lord, show your mercy.
For the hungry and the persecuted; for those sick in body or mind, let us pray to the Lord.
　Lord, show your mercy.
Let us commend ourselves and one another and our whole life to Christ, our God.
　To you, O Lord.
You have in your grace enabled us to offer prayers together and with one mind; and you have promised, when two or three agree in your name, to grant their requests; fulfil now the petitions of your servants, as you judge to be right; grant us in this world knowledge of your truth, and, in the world to come, eternal life.   Amen.

O, only begotten Son and Word of God, you who share for eternity the divine nature, yet who deigned for our salvation to be incarnate through your mother, the Virgin Mary,

Who was crucified on the Cross of Shame for our salvation,
Who rose victorious from death to overcome death,
Save us, O Christ, and make us worthy to serve you and the
world you came to redeem,
You, who in the Holy Trinity, are glorious with the Father
and the Holy Spirit.   Amen.
Liverpool Cathedral

213   An Act of Intercession for Christian Unity

Lord Jesus Christ, in you we see the Father's love – the love
he gives us in the Spirit – and in that love we pray
For all Christians: that they may renew their hope in the power
of your Father who loves the world and saves it;
For all men: that in the hour and by the means you choose,
you will unite them to yourself in love and truth.

> *O Lord hear our prayer*

May the Holy Spirit carry to the Father our prayer for unity:
Keep us, O Lord, from growing accustomed to our divisions.
Save us from considering as normal that which is a scandal to
the world and an offence against your love.

> *Unite us in love and in truth*

Deliver us, O Lord from a spirit of narrowness, of bitterness,
or of prejudice. Teach us to recognize the gifts of your grace
in all those who call upon you with an honest heart.

> *Unite us in love and in truth*

Deepen our faithfulness to your word. Do not allow us to be
led astray by our own delusions or to walk in paths which are
not of your choosing.

> *Unite us in love and in truth*

By thy power, O Lord, gather your scattered flock. Unite it
under the authority of your Son, so that the purpose of your
love may be fulfilled and that the world may know you, the
one true God, and him whom you have sent, Jesus Christ.
Amen.
Liverpool Cathedral

214   Church Councils

O Holy Spirit of God, we ask for your presence and guidance
at the meeting of the Church Council (*this week*). May each
member exercise his responsibilities wisely and prayerfully,
and may the decision of the council be in accordance with
your will and for the extension of Christ's kingdom in this
parish, for his name's sake.   Amen.
Peter Markby.

215   Heavenly Father, send your Holy Spirit to guide all members
of Church Councils. May all who are called to this work be
committed to serving and pleasing you, so that the work of
the Church in the world may be helped forward and not
hindered, through Jesus Christ our Lord.   Amen.
Joyce Francis

216   Before a Committee Meeting

Lord, guide us as we meet together that we may think calmly
and carefully, decide wisely and well, in order that
everything may be done in accordance with your will.
Help us to make your concerns our concerns, so that through
us you may be able to carry on your work here on earth, for
Jesus Christ's sake,
Amen.
John D. Searle

217   An Increase in Congregation

Heavenly Father, we continue to pray that you will multiply
the number of worshippers in your church of ———; that
they may be drawn together purely by love of yourself and
for your glory; that your love may become the mainspring of
their lives, so that they may show love to each other, and to
those around them. Change us who are praying into your
likeness, through the mighty love of your Son, Jesus Christ
our Lord.   Amen.
Henry Lambert-Smith

218   Building a new church

Almighty Father, who has set us the task of building a new
church in this parish, where generations yet unborn shall
worship you; look graciously upon our efforts, we beseech
you; inspire us by your Spirit, that we may not become
despondent, but may have faith to match all difficulties,
believing that in your strength we may soon lay its foundations
with joy, and build its walls in hope. We ask this through our
Lord and Saviour Jesus Christ.   Amen.
Henry Lambert-Smith

219   At an Ordination retreat

Lord, who commanded storm and tumult saying 'Peace, be
still', breathe stillness now to our expectant hearts. Help us to
rest upon your faithfulness, to receive the fullness of your love,
and to be at peace within ourselves as ministers whom Christ
has called; for his name's sake.   Amen.
Timothy Dudley-Smith

220   Grant, Lord, to those now called to ministry and service:
increasing knowledge of the living God,
confidence in the gospel and the Word of Life,
compassion for the lost and needy,
courage, endurance and
unfailing love.
For Jesus' sake.   Amen.
Timothy Dudley-Smith

MISSION
221   Missionary Meetings

Awaken every sense, O Lord, to your presence in our midst.
May our meeting together tonight be a meeting with you
and, if it is your will, make it as unforgettable for us as those
meetings with other disciples in Galilee long ago.
Therefore, Lord, bless those who speak in your name. Clothe
yourself in their thoughts, appear to us in their words. So
through the mystery of preaching, and in the ministry of

hearing, we may behold you in our midst; for your dear
name's sake.   Amen.
Dick Williams

222   Lord, look upon us this night, solitary grains of wheat
unwilling to die, but bearing within ourselves all that you
require to speak to the world, all you require to make yourself
known to mankind, all you require to cause such a light to
shine that every dark corner of creation might be illuminated
by the radiance of your love. So save us, Lord, from living for
ourselves, save us from abiding alone, imprisoned by our
fears, isolated by our ambitions, deformed by our conceit.
May the Spirit of Jesus move us to follow him; may the power
of the Cross make us take it up. Give us the power, and give
us the will, and give us the understanding to lay down our
life. So shall we be free from ourselves, free to live, and so
shall we bear much fruit, through Jesus Christ our Lord.
Amen.
Dick Williams

223   Almighty God, teach us afresh the meaning of almightiness.
Build into the fabric of our thought and feeling the certain
knowledge that whatever pit of evil opens at the feet of
mankind – whatever depth of sin draws men downward –
whatever obstacle to your love towers across the Christian's
path – in you are the resources to guide, to deliver, to
overcome.
Give us afresh the assurance of your almightiness. Give us
the mastery over every empire of the intellect which in the
name of truth assails the truth, teach us to out-think, out-
reason, out-debate and out-live the wisdom of this world.
But, by the cross of Jesus, renew in us the needful knowledge
that even almightiness cannot win the hearts of men except
through pain and grief. So teach us, Lord, and all the Church
militant, to know the conditions on which men receive God's
power, and help us, and the whole Church, to fulfil them,
through Jesus Christ our Lord.   Amen.
Dick Williams

224   We thank you, Lord, for all those who have seen Jesus in
their inner life, and who have given their lives as grains of
wheat to the soil of your good purposes. We thank you in
particular for all those who have done this in the fellowship
of (*name of missionary society*). Grant that they may all, day
by day, discover the almightiness of the Lord. Grant to them,
new every morning, the refreshing knowledge of your love,
the awareness of the wider Christian family whose life is
bound up in theirs, and holy communion with the life of
heaven which sustains us all. Graciously provide for all their
manifold needs of spirit, mind and body and circumstance;
and to all your servants in every land grant a fresh vision of
the Lord, a new willingness to lay down their life, and a never
ending discovery of your almightiness and your love. Through
Jesus Christ our Lord.   Amen.
Dick Williams

225   Sanctify our gathering together with your presence, O Lord.
May your Word quicken the words to be spoken; your
Spirit quicken the hearts that shall receive them, and your love
unite us in a community of loving concern; that the place
which this work has in your holy will and mighty purposes
might be faithfully mirrored in the life of your church. Through
Jesus Christ our Lord.   Amen.
Dick Williams

226   Missionaries

We thank you, Lord, for your special call to overseas service,
and for those who have answered it. We pray that their work
(in ——) may receive such blessing from you, that they may
serve you faithfully and also see some fruit from their labours:
that many (*in that land*) may be won from ignorance,
superstition and bondage, and brought into the light and
freedom of the good news of Jesus Christ: for his sake.
Amen.
Christopher Idle

227   We thank you, Father, for Jesus Christ our Lord, and for
giving his Church the work of spreading the gospel and
announcing his death and resurrection. Be with all who are
his witnesses: missionaries in other countries, ministers and
other workers in our land, youth leaders and teachers in day
school and Sunday School, and all Christians everywhere.
Make and keep them faithful to you, true to their message,
and full of love for the world and its people, for Jesus Christ's
sake.   Amen.

228   O God, your gospel has the strength to set free those who
are entangled and imprisoned by their own sins. Grant power
to every member of your Church that, being ambassadors for
Christ, they may so speak of him – crucified, risen and alive
today – that many may come to share in the glorious freedom
of your children; through the power of his name and for the
sake of his name.   Amen.
Christopher Idle

229   Missionary Families

O God our Father, you have told us of our great
responsibilities towards our children, and you have also told
us that if we love our children more than you, we are not
worthy of you. Guide missionary parents as they seek to
bring up their families, and surround the children with your
love, especially when they are at school far away from their
parents: for Jesus' sake.   Amen.
J. Wheatley Price

230   Missionaries

Heavenly Father, you who call men and women to preach
the unsearchable riches of Christ, be at this time with all those
known to us who are sharing with others this good news.
Be their companion in loneliness, their strength in weakness,
their inspiration when the work is hard or dull; and grant them
the joy of seeing the fruit of eternal life, both in themselves
and in others: for Jesus Christ's sake.   Amen.
J. Wheatley Price

231 Action

Almighty God, who told Abraham to leave home and to find
his security not in circumstances but in obedience, help us to
obey the commands which we have heard; to do what we
know to be right, and to leave the consequences to you; for
Jesus' sake. Amen.
J. Wheatley Price

232 Prophets

O God of the nations, when corruption abounds and
Christians grow cynical; when racialism is rampant and
Christians seek their own interests; when consciences are
stifled and it is safer to keep silent – call out your prophets.
Give them courage to speak, clarity in doing so, and a fire in
the belly, which will not let them be silent; by the power of
your Holy Spirit. Amen.
J. Wheatley Price

233 The Power to Communicate

Lord, may we find ways of communicating to others what is
in our hearts, through Jesus Christ our Lord. Amen.
J. R. Worsdall

234 Christians and Jews

Grant, O Lord, that your people of the Old Testament, and
your people of the New Testament might live together in
justice and harmony as children of the one God and Father
of all; for truth and mercy's sake. Amen.
We thank you, Lord God, for the mystery of your convenant
with the Children of Israel; for the commandments of your
law, and the sure word of prophecy proclaimed among
them for their good and for ours. We thank you for the
manifestation of your grace whereby the Word of both law
and prophecy was made flesh and dwelt among us in Jesus
Christ.
We pray that all people everywhere may look to you, O

Lord, who art the author of every good and perfect gift and
the creator and sustainer of our faith.
We thank you, Lord, for the nourishment you have provided
in the Scriptures to satisfy our thirsting souls. Together with
the prophet Isaiah we await the day when the earth shall be
full of the knowledge of the Lord as the waters cover
the sea.
Remove from the hearts of all Christians the ignorance,
apathy or prejudice which negates their gospel, and may the
whole Church be informed with a glad and lively
understanding of your will; through Jesus Christ our Lord.
Amen.
Dick Williams (adapted)

235   O God we thank you that in the days of old you called
your servant Abraham to go into an unknown land to worship
the true God and promised him that in his family all
people would find a blessing.
We thank you that Abraham left the security of his
homeland and followed your calling, becoming thereby an
example of faith for all generations. We pray that a faith
such as Abraham's might be kindled in the hearts of your
people today so that on this earth your will might be done
and your children blessed; in Jesus' name. Amen.
Walter Barker (adapted)

236   Forgive us, O Lord, because Christian people have so often
persecuted the Jews and have acted contrary to the spirit of
Christ. Bless all those who today, by word and deed, are
showing forth the healing love of Christ. Help each one
of us to do our part; in Jesus' name. Amen.
Walter Barker (adapted)

237   O God our Father, we thank you for inspiring Hebrew
writers to give us the Bible. We thank you for the Jewish
disciples who were the first missionaries and preachers of
the Good News. We thank you above all for Jesus, your Son,
who was born a Jew. Help us to repay so great a debt by

doing all we can to promote understanding and goodwill
between ourselves and the Jewish people. Amen.
Walter Barker (adapted)

238   The Church in Closed Lands

O Lord Jesus Christ, you who open so that none shall shut,
and shut so that none shall open: we cry to you for your own
people in those countries which men have tried to close to
your voice. We thank you that they are open to your Spirit
and your love; to the message of the Bible which cannot be
bound, and to the Church which cannot die. We pray that you
will strengthen this part of your Church. Grant to its leaders
and all its members a new reliance on you to whom all power
is given, and a new commitment of themselves to share the
gospel with others before it is too late: for the sake of your
kingdom and your glory.   Amen.
Christopher Idle (slightly adapted)

239   Christians Whose Faith is Attacked

Heavenly Father, we thank you that through the faithful
witness of Christians from other lands the gospel was brought
to this country and that it has been passed on to each
successive generation and so to us. Bless those who do not
have this heritage or who lack the freedom to enjoy it, and
make your presence and our prayers very real to those who
live in countries where the faith is suppressed, that seeing him
who is invisible they may endure.   Amen.
Patricia Mitchell (adapted)

240   Different Religions

Heavenly Father, help us to be willing to learn more about the
world's religions, so that we may understand our differences
and share our common convictions, and go forward in faith
to learn more of the truth as it is revealed in Jesus Christ our
Lord.   Amen.
Joyce Francis (adapted)

241   Understanding Other Religions

Lord of all truth, make us sensitive and humble in our approach
to all men. As we learn of their search for truth within the
terms of other religions, help us also to see your search for
them. Grant that by your Spirit, and through the obedience of
your disciples, what they have learned of you and your love
may find its fulfilment in Christ, through whom alone we come
to the full knowledge of yourself: God blessed forever.   Amen.
Alan Nugent

242   Understanding Secular Man

Lord of all truth, make us sensitive and humble in our
approach to modern secular men. Help us to understand his
confusion, and appreciate his quest. Help us to respond to his
cry and serve him with care and understanding. May your
Holy Spirit so guide us to interpret your truth that many may
come to find in you their purpose, their meaning and their
life: through Jesus Christ our Lord.   Amen.
Alan Nugent

243   Nations under Communist or other Dictatorships

We plead with you today, O God, for those nations under
Communist rule, and others in East and West where totalitarian
governments give little freedom:
For their leaders we ask that they may learn to govern in
justice, mercy and truth;
For their people, we ask that they may be able to hear your
gospel and heed your word;
And for all your servants in these lands, we pray for great
faithfulness, great courage, and great love; through Jesus
Christ our Lord.   Amen.
Christopher Idle

244   Missionary Societies in a New Age

We thank you Lord, that the dream of missionaries of old has
in part been realized and that your church has been planted in
every land. Help the missionary societies of our church to

understand your will for the whole church in this new age,
and direct them into the work which shall express it. And as
we thank you for the dedication of the pioneers of
missionary endeavour we pray that your Church, under the
guidance of the Holy Spirit, may face the challenges of a
different world order still looking for the day when your
kingdom shall be acknowledged in the lives of all men:
through Jesus Christ our Lord.   Amen.
Alan Nugent

245   Parish Missions

Risen Lord Jesus, we remember the way in which you called
the disciples to be with you, and recall how you sent them
out, two by two, invested with your authority to speak about
God, and your power to cast out of men's hearts all that
makes for death and destruction. Bless our desire to bring
your message to this parish. Help us first to dwell with you,
and may it be your voice in our hearts which shall bid us go
forth. And just as you rejoiced at the simplicity of your first
disciples, and through this saw the power of darkness fall, so
give to us that uncomplicated response of children which you
have taught us is the supreme achievement of the adult soul;
for your dear name's sake.   Amen.
Dick Williams

246   Eternal God, you who have formed the universe and
breathed life into mankind; call out from your Church men
and women to serve you in the world. Equip them with the
gifts of your Holy Spirit and entrust to them the great task of
bringing new life to the deadness which surrounds us; that
there may be a new creation in the hearts of all who turn to
your Son in repentance and faith. It is in his name, O God,
that we bring our prayer.   Amen.
Michael Saward

247   O Lord Jesus Christ, you have commanded us to preach the
Good News to all men; bless us as we do so here, in your
name. Move, we pray you, the hearts of all who profess that
name to join us in that task; and hasten the coming of your

kingdom; O Lord and Saviour who with the Father and
the Holy Spirit, lives and reigns one God, for ever and
ever.
C. O'C. Davies

248   Zeal in Personal Evangelism

O living Lord, traveller in the way of men, our trail blazer
into eternity: kindle in our hearts the passionate fire of
heaven. Burn from our mind the dross of this world's thinking;
so may we dare to imitate your love, and, risking all through
your emboldening, dare to share your truth at all times and in
all ways, bringing glory to your name.   Amen.
Alan Godson

249   What are we for, creator infinite, if not to show your likeness
unto men, introducing godliness into manhood, life into death:
may we not hide you by our ways, nor cover your reality with
our fears. May hungry hearts which long for purpose find
their joy because you meet men not in the past alone, but in
their present deeds for which you did atone. Save, Lord!
Then, bringer back from death, we salute you till you come.
Amen.
Alan Godson

250   Camps and Retreats

We commend to you, Lord, all the members of this and other
churches who come together in Christian camps and retreats:
to those who lead them as counsellors and teachers, give
wisdom, patience, efficiency and love; to all adults, youth,
and children, give health, safety and enjoyment; that every
one of them may be getting to know you better, and that
the eyes of some may be opened for the first time to your
gift of eternal life in Jesus your Son: for his name's sake.
Amen.
Christopher Idle

251 Evangelistic Meetings

God of grace and mercy, open the eyes of the blind this
night: breathe life upon the dead this night; release those who
are bound by death and Satan; and may the Holy Spirit take
the truths of Christ and impress them upon our hearts, our
minds, our wills: that hearts may be moved, minds convinced,
and wills challenged, in his name. Amen.
Michael Saward

252 Missionary Power

O risen Christ
Whose wounds declare the suffering and the victory of God:
We thank you for bursting the bonds of death.
Look at us now.
Look at *our* bonds.
Look at the things which tie us down,
Which fasten our hands and hobble our feet,
Which stop us from walking in your ways,
Which stop us from doing your works,
Which tether us so tightly to the dead weight of past failures.
And as you have burst the bonds of death
So burst these bonds and set us free.
Set us free from our pride; set us free from our sin;
Set us free from our fear; set us free from ourselves.
Stand in our midst, and in our hearts let us behold you.
Lay on us your hands. Breathe into us your breath.
Speak to us and may your speech be written into the beating
of our hearts.
Speak to us and may your speech be carried in the motions
of our mind.
So may the fire of your life fall upon us,
That we may have faith to move the mountains of
irrelevance in our churches,
And may have that love without which faith is vain.
So give us speech that each man may hear us speak in his own
tongue.
So give us life that we may fashion anew in this generation
That army of disciples which can win the world for you.

Look at us, Lord...
And may this body which you have bought by your death
Now be occupied by your resurrection, and filled with your
spirit:
For your glory – for our peace – for the world – and for
yourself. Amen.
Dick Williams

253   Asia

O God, who called wise men from the East to bring their
treasures to the feet of Christ: Grant that the men of Asia
may see a new star and set out on a new pilgrimage, so may
they and all mankind meet at the feet of Christ: for his name's
sake. Amen.
Dick Williams

254   As we think of the people of Eastern Asia we reaffirm our
faith in one God who made of one blood all men everywhere.
Through Jesus Christ, made man, living as a Jew in a Roman
world, we pray for them and for ourselves:
We pray that by every practical means understanding may
grow and the love of God be seen:
through exchange visits;
international students;
the United Nations;
Church conferences;
pen friends;
missionaries;
through literature, radio and television;
by imagination, faith and prayer.
We confess it is often difficult to love and hard to understand
those who seem to belong to another world.
God save us from easy talk about brotherhood, and hollow
charity;
Save us from the hardness of prejudice, and from not trying
to understand.
We confess our need and our desire to learn and grow with
them,

that we may together be filled with the Spirit of Jesus, and his gifts of love and joy and peace.   Amen.
Simon H. Baynes

255 Africa

O God our Father, who gave to a man of Africa the privilege of carrying the cross of Jesus: give courage to the Christians of Africa when they walk the road of ridicule and suffering. Build a Church which is not ashamed of Jesus Christ, Christ nailed to the cross: for his name's sake.   Amen.
J. Wheatley Price

THE SICK AND SUFFERING
256 A Nurse's Verse

Lord of all our aches and pain
Help us so to use the brain
Thou gavest us, that we may share
The pain which others have to bear,
Thus linking them to us and thee,
Thyself the Watch...
Help us to be minutes of thy time.

Grant Lord that we may bless
The hours when we receive
Rest from thy hands
And peaceful sleep.
We thank thee, Lord,
And vigil keep.
Lucy Smith

257 Physically Handicapped People

One day we shall understand, O Lord, why some are physically handicapped while others walk and run, and why life should be this way. But on the path to truth, dear God, teach us to help the afflicted and let their patience, hope and love, spread over our embittered world; through Jesus Christ our Lord.   Amen.
based on a prayer by Susan Heywood

258   Transplant Surgery

O God, our heavenly Father, creator of our bodies and of all
that exists; we thank you for the knowledge and skill of
surgeons and doctors, and for the advances that have been
made in combating disease. We pray that all those in the
forefront of medical and surgical research may be guided both
in the practical and ethical aspects of their work. May the
good of the patients never be sacrificed for the sake of prestige
or any other unworthy cause. May the side effects and
complications induced by some new treatments be seen and
overcome. May all be done in the spirit of him who went about
healing all manner of sickness and disease among the people,
your Son, Jesus Christ our Lord.   Amen.
Andrew Warner

259   Thanksgiving for our Bodies

O God our heavenly Father, we thank you for the wonderful
way our bodies are made. We praise you for each breath we
take, each step we take; for the gift of sight and the power to
read; for the minds that can observe and store up what they
see. We thank you for hands that are skilful in doing work,
and for all the creative arts within us. And above all we praise
you that our bodies are the temples of your own Spirit and
that we are made in your image. Father we give you praise;
through Christ our Lord.   Amen.
Patricia Mitchell

260   Those in Distress

Dear Lord, please comfort and sustain all those in dire distress
and give to us all strength in our weakness, courage in defeat,
wisdom in perplexity and patience under provocation. Make us
true where we are false, and above all so fill our hearts with
loving kindness that there shall be in them no room for any
uncharitable thought. O Lord help us all who need your help
so much. Amen.
Marjorie Hay

261   The Aged

We pray, Lord, for those who have outlived the resources of
their mind or body and for whom age is a burden and a
sorrow. Help them to know your presence in their need.
Assure them afresh that in Christ their spirits may live more
ardently than ever. And enable them, through loving you, to
be a blessing to others, and particularly to those who have the
care of them. Grant them to know that while you call them to
remain on earth there is a purpose in their life and a grace for
their living: through Jesus Christ our Lord.   Amen.
Dick Williams

262   The Housebound

O Lord Jesus Christ, the help of the helpless and
companion of the lonely: we ask you to bless all those who
are unable to leave their homes or to join in public worship.
Grant that they may always be confident of your presence
with them, and of their oneness with the whole family of
your church; and grant that with one mind and one voice we
all may worship you O Christ who, with the Father and the
Spirit, reigns for evermore.   Amen.
Andrew Warner

263   Thanksgiving For Those Made Well

We join today in thanking you, Lord, with all who have been
restored again to better health;
for faith and patience granted to us;
for healing in body, mind and spirit;
for the skill and friendship and generosity of others;
for the possibility of prayer and the comfort of the Bible;
for sins forgiven and pardon assured;
and through it all for your unfailing presence, we give you
thanks and praise, through Jesus Christ our Lord.   Amen.
Christopher Idle

264   The Suffering

We thank you Father that out of suffering can spring
compassion and caring, faith and endurance; joy from getting
to know you; humility in knowing that you suffered too. We
bring before you now all those known to us who are in any
kind of need. Give them courage and let your peace be in
them; through Jesus Christ our Lord.   Amen.
Patricia Mitchell

265   O Lord, we beseech you to strengthen those in pain and
comfort those in sorrow and may the Spirit of Jesus, the great
physician both of body and soul, be present in our parish, in
our hospitals, and in the world.   Amen.
Simon H. Baynes

266   O God, the source of life and health, we pray for all who are
ill. Give doctors and nurses skill to make them well again,
and grant that during their illness they may learn more of
your love and care; through Jesus Christ our Lord.   Amen.
M. H. Botting's collection

267   Merciful Father, help all who suffer pain of body or grief of
heart, to find in you their help; and as Jesus suffered pain in
his body and healed it in others, help them to find their peace
in him, and by your mercy be renewed in strength of body
and mind. Through Jesus Christ our Lord.   Amen.
Dick Williams

268   The Mentally Ill

O God, the maker of men's minds and healer of their ills:
bless all your children who suffer from mental illness; help
them to trust you even on the darkest days; help them to
know you in their deepest need, and in your mercy release
them from the causes of their sickness, that they may love and
serve you with all their strength, with all their heart, and with
all their mind; through Jesus Christ our Lord.   Amen.
Dick Williams

269   O Lord Jesus Christ, by whom one who wandered among
the tombs was once healed and clothed and converted: we
pray for your gift of mental health for those who suffer in
mind, for any reason and to any degree. Grant them release
from the tyranny of themselves, to enjoy the freedom and
power of a character made complete by knowing you.
And to those who care for them and try to cure them, give
wisdom, skill and unfailing love; for your own name's sake.
Amen.
Christopher Idle

270   **People Who Are Depressed**

O Lord, who shouldered the strain and the stress of life, be
with those who because of their burdens go down into the pit
of disturbance and depression. When things are black and
hopeless stretch out your hand to hold them firm. Give them
courage to climb upwards to the light of this world's day, and
of your love; through Jesus Christ our Lord.   Amen.
Marjorie Hampson

271   **Psychiatrists and Those Who Fight Mental Disease**

Lord of all power and might, bless those who try to heal the
disordered minds of men. Teach them first to study the mind
of Christ, and inspire them to love this study best of all; and
in their exploration of the minds of men help them to be so
secure in their own grasp upon reality, that their strength of
will, soundness of purpose, and wholeness of spirit, may
sustain them in their toil and give them good success; through
Jesus Christ our Lord.   Amen.
Dick Williams

272   **The Elderly**

Eternal God, whose Son Jesus Christ is the same yesterday,
today and forever: we pray in his name for all who can now
look back over many years of change, times of sadness and
times of joy:
to those with a true sense of achievement in their lives grant

the willingness to give you the glory;
to those with a sense of disappointment give the faith that
your mercies are new every morning;
to those who have lost their faith and are lonely, grant the
strengthening of their friendship with Christ;
to those who are losing their health or their faculties, grant
the knowledge that their prayers are precious to you, and the
grace to accept what seems too hard;
to those who can still influence others, grant youthfulness of
mind and spirit, that their experience may be welcomed and
valued;
and to those who are facing eternity very soon, grant the
confidence to place their hands in the hand once pierced with
nails, and now stretched out to meet them, the hand of him
who died and rose and is alive forever, even Jesus Christ
your Son our Lord.   Amen.
Christopher Idle

273   The Bereaved

We remember, Lord, the slenderness of the thread which
separates life from death, and the suddenness with which it
can be broken. Help us also to remember that on both sides
of that division we are surrounded by your love. Persuade our
hearts that when our dear ones die neither we nor they are
parted from you. In you may we find our peace and in you be
united with them in the glorious body of Christ, who has burst
the bonds of death and is alive for evermore, our saviour and
theirs for ever and ever.   Amen.
Dick Williams

274   O God our Father, we pray for those whose life is saddened
by the death of a relative or friend. Be with them in their
loneliness, and give them faith to look beyond their present
trouble to Jesus, the one who died and rose again, and who
lives for evermore.   Amen.
M. H. Botting's collection

275 Ourselves as Healers

Dear Master, who neither slumbers nor sleeps, we thank you
for your protecting care through the night watches, and for the
dawn of a new day. Create in us a clean heart, and make us to
resemble you. Our life is like the loaves and fishes brought to
you to feed five thousand. Multiply and magnify our life that
through prayer and rich self-giving we may feed multitudes.
Touch us before the hurrying world touches us, so that the
fever of restlessness may leave us and we may minister to
others with a still heart. Today our life may be the only Bible
some may read; make it a story of love and service for the
great physician. May the lonely, homesick, needy ones reach
from the crowd and touch the hem of your garment. And may
we carry cups of water for your dear name's sake. For tonight
we may hear you say 'Inasmuch as you have done it to one of
these, you have done it to me'. Lord hear our prayer, for your
dear name's sake.   Amen.
adapted from a prayer by B. Thornton

276 After a Disaster

Lord of compassion and power, be with those who have
survived this disaster: minister to their needs of mind and
spirit, body and circumstance; heal those who are hurt; give
peace to the dying; comfort and support the bereaved; and to
all who are working to bring relief and restore order, give
strength and resilience to do their work well; for the sake of
Jesus Christ our Lord.   Amen.
Dick Williams

277 Those in Trouble

Almighty and ever loving God, the comfort of the sad, the
strength of the suffering: let the prayers of all who cry out of
any tribulation come unto you; and to every soul that is
distressed grant mercy, refreshment and peace; for the sake of
Jesus Christ our Lord.   Amen.
Margaret Girdlestone

278   The Broken Hearted

'The Lord is near to the broken hearted and saves the crushed
in spirit' (Psalm 34.18).
Let us pray for broken homes; teenagers torn by doubts and
disillusionment; old people bewildered by infirmities and lack
of contact; sick people fearful of the future; those who mourn.
Lord, on behalf of all people in distress, especially those known
to us,
We claim your promise that you are near to the broken
hearted and save the crushed in spirit. Use us as channels of
your healing power. We thank you, Lord.   Amen.
Patricia Mitchell

THE UNDERPRIVILEGED
279   The Starving World

Dear Lord, look down upon the starving world, your world;
the homeless men, the widowed women, the children
desperate for bread. Lord Jesus, take and save and feed us all.
Pour down your manna, your love, your life, yourself. Have
pity upon those who fast: have pity on us who feast. Pity
them the pitiful, and us the pitiless. Have mercy on their
starving bodies and our starving souls.   Amen.
Simon H. Baynes

280   Have mercy, O Lord our God, on those whom war,
oppression or famine has robbed of homes and friends. Guide
us and all men as we seek to show them the love of Christ by
our prayerful concern and practical action; for his sake.   Amen.
M. H. Botting's collection

281   Relief Work

Forgive us, Father, that we are so eager to make our own
lives comfortable whilst others must suffer hunger and want.
Bless the little which we have done and multiply it, in your
mercy, to serve the needs of many unknown to us, but known
and loved by you. May some give thanks to you, as we do,

for all your love and care; through Jesus Christ our Lord.
Amen.
Ian D. Bunting

282   Deprived and Suffering People

Grant to your afflicted children, O Lord, patience under their
sufferings, discipline in their affairs, hope in their hearts, peace
in their minds; and grant to us who have enough of this
world's goods, so to share our substance and our skills, that
in our day and age we may see all men enter fully into the
inheritance which is their birthright; through Jesus Christ
our Lord.   Amen.
Dick Williams

283   For the Hungry

For all who are starving, O God, we ask your saving grace.
Move us to answer our own prayer at least in part by giving
money to those now trying to bring them practical help.
Move the governments of the world to plan wisely and
generously for the long term relief of all such chronic
injustice, and strengthen and inspire all whose lives are spent
in bringing first aid food to mankind maimed by hunger;
through Jesus Christ our Lord.   Amen.
Dick Williams

284   For the Needy

Almighty Father, giver of life and health, we beseech you for
the millions of people who suffer from hunger. We
acknowledge the richness of your bounty towards us, and we
pray for grace to show our thankfulness by seeking to relieve
the needs of those who are in want. We ask this in the name
of him who is the bread of life, your Son, Jesus Christ our
Lord.   Amen.
Bernard Woolf

285

We cry to you, O Saviour, for the homeless and the
hopeless; for those who have no work, no clothes, or no food.
We cannot always hear their cries; but you can hear them,

even when they do not know to whom they cry. We pray that
you will be with them to rescue them, and that you will be
with us to drive us to their aid; for your own name's sake.
Amen.
Christopher Idle

286 O God, whose nature it is to be generous: we confess to you
our share of the guilt for a world of hungry families and
homeless peoples; forgive us for our lack of concern for them;
forgive us for our self-centred living and spending; forgive
those who blame you for their failures. Grant that this week
some who have given nothing may start to give; those who
have given something may give more; that both our church
and our nation may give due place to the cries of those who
have nothing to eat and nowhere to live; for the sake of Jesus
Christ.   Amen.
Christopher Idle

287 **Refugees**

O Lord, have pity on those today who live in stables as you
did, and those who because of persecution take refuge in
another land. We know you care for them, because you
yourself were once one of them. Help us to care too, and so
fulfil the law of Christ.   Amen.
Simon H. Baynes

288 Lord, make us more thankful for what we have received;
make us more content with what we have; and make us more
mindful of other people in need. We ask it for the sake of him
who lived in poverty, our Saviour, Jesus Christ.   Amen.
Simon H. Baynes

289 **The Victims of Vandalism and Crime**

In this world we live in, the violence of a few strikes random
victims amongst the many. We lift up before the Lord these
victims, remembering all those who have been physically hurt;
all those who have been robbed of personal treasures; all

those who suffer reactions of bitterness and fear.

O Lord, Jesus Christ, whose perfect love met death by violence
and was not extinguished: so enter the hearts and minds of
all victims that frailty may give way to your strength, loss to
your gain, bitterness to your total and victorious love; for your
name's sake. Amen.

Susan Williams

290   Stewardship

O God, rich in mercy, whose Son showed how hard it is for
rich men to enter your kingdom; guard us from the
temptation to use money wrongly; save us from selfishness,
carelessness and waste; deliver us from the love of money
which is the root of all evil; help us to use properly what has
been entrusted to us; to spend wisely and to save wisely, that
neither poverty nor riches may hinder our Christian
discipleship. And for those who have large sums to handle
and great policies to decide, we ask that you will make them
efficient, fair, and strong to resist temptation; through Jesus
Christ our Saviour.   Amen.

Christopher Idle

291   Lord Jesus Christ, you have taught us that we cannot love God
and money, and that all our possessions are a trust from you.
Teach us to be faithful stewards of our time, our talents, and
our money, that we may help others and extend your kingdom;
for your name's sake.   Amen.

M. H. Botting's collection

292   Immigrants

O God of all the nations upon earth, show us how to use our
country for the benefit of mankind. Make our hearts to be sound
in love and truth. Guide those who frame our laws. Teach us
how to integrate into our society people from other lands.
And may no difficulty blind us to the value of every human
being, declared by Christ, and written into history by his
blood, for whose sake we pray.   Amen.

after Andrew Warner

293   O God, whose only Son was an immigrant into this world,
       bless all who move from the land of their birth to live in
       another. Guard and guide those who go from this land to live
       overseas. Guard and guide those who come from distant
       countries to live in this. And may loved ones abroad, and
       strangers at home, all be enabled to form new friendships and
       build a new world, through him who makes all things new,
       even Jesus Christ our Saviour and our Lord.   Amen.
       Dick Williams

SOCIETY
294   **The Society in Which We Live**

       'Let justice roll down like waters, and righteousness like an
       everflowing stream.'
       O God of love, who has always required that humans be
       just: forgive us for complacency and lack of care; for burying
       our heads in welfare programs and believing all is well
       with the poor, the hungry, and the handicapped. In a society
       where those who shout loudest are best rewarded, open our
       eyes to the injustice around us, and help us to give up
       ourselves, our time, our comfort and our possessions, in the
       service of others and of yourself; through Jesus Christ our
       Lord. Amen.
       Susan Williams

295   **Employers**

       Lord Jesus, we ask you to give to all employers the
       strength to cope with the problems and difficulties inherent
       in their job. Give them the grace to listen patiently, see things
       clearly and act with wisdom, and help them to show your
       understanding and justice to all men; for your name's sake.
       Amen.
       W. A. Hampson

296   **Shop Stewards**

       Lord Jesus, you once worked with your hands at the
       carpenter's bench and you know the difficulties of men

employed in industry today. We ask you to be with their
shop stewards. Keep them always close to you and let their
minds be in tune with yours. May they see the problems
clearly and try to solve them as you would have done; for
your name's sake.   Amen.
W. A. Hampson

297   Daily Work

O Lord Jesus Christ, you were a craftsman working at the
carpenter's bench. Help all workmen to be as good as you
were. Give them pride in their work. Let them not be content
to turn out a shoddy job. Help them to be completely honest,
not always watching the clock, or being more concerned in
how much they can get. When the job is monotonous, help
them to remember that each job well done is a job done for
you; for your name's sake.   Amen.
W. A. Hampson

298   The Social Services

We thank you, O God, for all who work in the social services:
for policemen and probation officers; for youth club leaders
and school teachers; for welfare workers and psychiatric
social workers, for doctors and nurses and many others. We
pray that you will give to all such people sympathy and
understanding, love and firmness, and the deep knowledge
that Jesus Christ is the only one who can make men truly
whole. We ask this for the sake of Jesus Christ, our Saviour
and our Lord.   Amen.
Peter Markby

299   We praise you, O Lord, for the Christian heritage of this
country, where those in the public service may help us to
share our burdens and our gifts. We praise you for those who
are called to social work for their career, and those who give
their spare time to care for others.
Be with those who try to repair broken lives and broken
homes; those who help prisoners and alcoholics; those who

work among young people in the grip of drugs; those who
help others to help themselves.
We pray that this work may be acceptable to you in Christ, and
that you will grant a true faith in him among those who serve
and those who are served; for his name's sake.   Amen.
Christopher Idle

300   Drugs: a thanksgiving

O God, who created the raw material of drugs not to cause
suffering but to relieve it: we give thanks for all medicines,
and for the inspiration and skill of those who discover and
administer them. We thank you for the relief from pain
brought by powerful drugs, and the psychiatric insights
secured by the proper use of others. In our concern about their
misuse may we never fail to thank you for the good which
drugs can do; through Christ the healer of men.
Andrew Warner (adapted)

301   For Drug Addicts

O Lord Jesus Christ, who came not to condemn the world
but to save men: look in mercy upon all drug addicts. Forgive
the actions which have brought them into captivity. Release
them from the thought of their next dose. Give them the will
to accept a cure where such is possible, and restore to them
the possibility of a healthy life; through Jesus Christ our Lord.
Amen.
Andrew Warner (adapted)

302   In every shabby room,
In every shabby street,
Where the junkie plays the game
and pays in blood to his high priest pusher to worship his
god, the drug:
Be present, Lord, to save.
And help us, Lord, to help the weak;
And to us all give strength and courage to learn to follow you;
through Jesus Christ our Lord.   Amen.
based on a prayer by Susan Heywood

303   Those Tempted to Take Drugs

Bless, O Lord, all who are tempted to take drugs: help them
to realize that not all experience is good, that not all
examples are to be followed, that not all pleasures herald joy
and bring enrichment. Give them a true knowledge of what
addiction really means, and above all give them such an
experience of yourself and your love that they will want no
artificial substitute; through Jesus Christ our Lord.   Amen.
Andrew Warner (adapted)

304   Lord Jesus Christ, you have promised perfect liberty to those
who trust you; we cry to you for those who are at this moment
enslaved by their own need of drugs.
Raise up men and women with the skills to assist them, and
give them the care they need;
Turn back those young people who have already begun the
drift towards addiction;
Help us to see how we may bear one another's burdens;
And for those for whom treatment has come too late grant
your mercy, the awareness of sin, the awareness of yourself,
and peace at the last.   Amen.
Christopher Idle

305   For the Unemployed in Winter

We commend to you, Father of mercies, all who will suffer
this winter through unemployment; all who would work if
they could, but whose labour seems not to be needed.
Provide, we pray, for them and their families; grant that no
bitterness of mind may blot out your love from their lives;
and help those in authority to give them the means of earning
their living again.
For the sake of that workman who was your only Son, Jesus
our living Saviour.   Amen.
Christopher Idle

306 City Vagabonds

We remember the vagabonds of our city, Lord: those who
scavenge through rubbish bins and sleep on steps in dark
corners; those who cannot or will not accept official aid. May
our love of cleanness and stability not close our mind to such
people. Help us to find feelings other than fear or disgust.
Help us to find a place for them other than the street. And
where official help fails may the Church of Christ succeed;
for Jesus' sake.   Amen.
after Elizabeth Houghton

307 For Drop-outs

O strong Son of God, who came to set men free; be with
those who falsely worship freedom; save them from the
slavery of self-regard; conquer their hearts, make them your
willing slaves; and so grant them the great freedom for which
they were made; for your great name's sake.   Amen.
Dick Williams

308 For Vandals

O God, we thank you for the beauty and health which exists
in the middle of cities.
We pray for those who cause senseless destruction; for
vandals who destroy the beauty of flowers, and destroy the
health of the community by wrecking property, creating
anger, suffering and suspicion.
Forgive us, Lord, for our own disobedience: we, whose instinct
it is to condemn, when your command is to forgive.
Forgive, Lord, all those whose lives have been bent by
ugliness, lack of love and lack of purpose, until the urge to
create has become the urge to destroy.
Forgive us, Lord, for our part in permitting the evils of the
city and the evils of the big estate, and help us to share with
others that power which can alone transform the human spirit
and make it gloriously yours; through Jesus Christ our Lord.
Amen.
Susan Williams

309 Deprived Young People

Father of purity and light
Goodness and love
With whom there are no shades of grey
Or passing shadows:
We bring before you many young people
Who by accident of birth
Live often in the shadows;
Some without a father
Some with parents who are mentally ill
Some bursting with stifled intelligence
Some innocently caught up with a bad gang
Those in detention
Those who are slaves to drink or drugs
From an early age.
Father of light
Allow that great light to shine through us
On the people who walk in darkness.
Through Jesus Christ
The Light of the World.   Amen.
Eddie Neale

310 Children Who Lack Love

Look in mercy, O Lord, upon all children born and reared in
families where they are not loved; upon all who for lack of
human love grow up unable to believe that God is love; upon
all unable to view society aright, for lack of love; for all who
are destructive in their deeds in order to exact their vengeance
or to cry for help. And grant that the Christ who won the
hearts of children, the hearts of parents, and the heart of a
dying thief, may win his victory in the hearts of all men
everywhere; for his great mercy's sake.   Amen.
Dick Williams

311 Those Living in Poor Homes

Lord of Glory
Who for our sakes became poor
Born in a back-yard stable
Laid gently in a feeding trough full of straw
We bring to the heart of your compassion
Those who live in much worse squalor today,
Squalor which insults the dignity you gave to man:
The old lady whose bed is surrounded
By pans half full of water
Lying amongst the raindrops
Which pierce her roof.
The family in the slum
Whose children sleep in the drawers of an old chest.
And the millions throughout the world
Who live in shanty towns or worse
Without water taps or sewers.
Lord of Glory
Give us the Spirit of your love
Never to rest complacent in our luxury
But to care... and to care...and to care...
For your glory.   Amen.
Eddie Neale

312 Boredom

O God, who made us in your image and set us in your
world, who makes each life a sphere of endless interest, and
calls us to explore a universe of marvellous diversity; we
confess the sins that lead to boredom; we lament the
selfishness which cuts us off from all that stimulates and
renews us; we seek to understand why we build boredom into
our industrial work; we wish to discover the pressures which
produce towns which are tedious to live in. Help us in all we
do to seek first your kingdom and your righteousness: in our
personal lives, in the planning of industry, the design of
towns, the development of culture, and the ordering of our
world; that being caught up in your great purposes, and having
great goals to strive for, our imaginations, our affections and

our wills might spring to endless life in that service for which
we were born, through Jesus Christ our Lord.   Amen.
Dick Williams

313   Those Living in Tall Blocks of Flats

Almighty God
When we see people living in accommodation
Which is little better than chickens in a battery farm
We know that you
Who created man with the stamp of your image
Cannot be satisfied.
Lord, it is true that we spoil our environment
All the time with our selfishness and sinfulness
But we pray that you will give
Architects and planners vision
And local authorities imagination
To recreate an environment
In which men will not be stifled
But set free to be fully the people
You always wanted them to be
Through the love of Jesus Christ.   Amen.
Eddie Neale

314   Redevelopment of Old Residential Areas

Loving Father, you know our feelings as we watch the dust
blow through empty houses, windowless buildings once warm
with family life; you know the heartbreaks caused as busy
streets turn cold and bleak, ravaged by vandals, destroyed by
progress.
Now, as the community crumbles before our very eyes, as
blueprints gain the upper hand, and the compulsory purchase
wins the day, we need the strong assurance of your care.
Grant that as the houses tremble and tumble we may know that

your love and faithfulness stand firm and abiding. Help us to
know that you love and care for us. And help us, for our part,
to understand, to care and to be concerned. So may you turn
destruction to your praise and make this community live again,
through Jesus Christ our Lord.   Amen.
A. E. Wells

315   Problem Families

Father
We bow low before you
From whom every family in heaven and on earth is named.
And we bring to you those families who have been unable
to cope with the pressures of modern life
Whose children go around in rags
And who sell the clothes they are given
Who can never afford to pay the rent or the electricity bills
Who are spurned by their neighbours
Who resort to sex fantasies and crimes
And who try to escape the hell they have made for
themselves by committing suicide.
So many tragedies like this, Father,
In this brutal world of ours
And they seem a long, long way
From their divine origin and destiny.
Fill us with shame for the sin
which wreaks such havoc with your creation
And fill us with love
Which overflows into the lives of others
And brings with it the patience
To withstand being hurt time and time again
For the sake of your Name.   Amen.
Eddie Neale

316 Meditation and Prayer for Those Tempted to Commit Suicide

(Matthew 11.28)
We remember in the presence of God
Our neighbours who find no purpose in life and no joy in living.
Jesus said
> *Come unto me.*

In the name of Jesus the crucified
We try to imagine the mood of despair
And the hatred of one's own body
Which makes men long for death.
Jesus said
> *Come unto me.*

Many of us have known such moods from time to time.
Perhaps some of us have been near to suicide itself.
Let us be honest with ourselves and with God.
And in our heart of hearts admit to him what we painfully try to forget.
Jesus said
> *Come unto me.*

With ourselves let us include in loving prayer
Those we may never meet and do not know
Who hate what they have done or what they are
And who cannot face life any more;
Many in our own community, our own street, in our own church.
Jesus said
> *Come unto me.*

Lord God, with us or without us,
By your word or by your deed,
Save, and redeem and give them your new life today.   Amen.
Simon H. Baynes

317 A Confession of Social Failure

The confusion of morals.
> *O Lord, forgive.*

The breakdown of social restraints
> *O Lord, forgive.*

The increase of crime and violence
> *O Lord, forgive.*

The commercialization of sex
> *O Lord, forgive.*

The traffic in drugs
> *O Lord, forgive.*

The exploitation of the teenager
> *O Lord, forgive.*

The apathy and disenchantment of young people
> *O Lord, forgive.*

Our loss of vision
> *O Lord, forgive.*

Our moral cowardice
> *O Lord, forgive.*

Our failure as parents and adults
> *O Lord, forgive.*

Our self seeking and self indulgence.
> *O Lord, forgive.*

Our love of money and possessions
> *O Lord, forgive.*

Our connivance at dishonesty and corruption
> *O Lord, forgive.*

Our unwillingness for service and self sacrifice.
> *O Lord, forgive.*

Liverpool Cathedral

318   For Those in Need

Let us pray for all threatened by war, famine or pestilence; for the work of relief organizations, and all who seek to conquer poverty and distress in the developing countries of Asia and Africa. Help us to see the poverty that exists in the midst of plenty in our own society. Give us a heart to understand human need, an eye to see it, and a will to serve our fellow men.

O Lord, hear our prayer
> *And let our cry come unto thee.*

Let us pray for all prisoners: that those deprived of their
liberty may find true freedom in thee; and for all young people
in distress and confusion, that thy way may be made known
to them. Grant that those who administer and interpret the
law may know Christ's law of love.
O Lord, hear our prayer
And let our cry come unto thee.
Let us pray for all immigrants and travellers; that they may
meet friendship and hospitality; for all who are homeless and
wandering, that they may find a true home in thee; for all
families without homes of their own, or in temporary
accommodation, that they may find a secure way of life.
O Lord, hear our prayer
And let our cry come unto thee.
Let us pray for the sick in body and the sick in mind: that
through thy healing power they may be made whole; for the
disabled and handicapped, that they may have faith and
courage in their daily lives; for frail and infirm old people,
that they may renew their strength by waiting upon thee;
and for the dying, that they may know peace at the last.
O Lord, hear our prayer
And let our cry come unto thee.
Let us pray for those who through sin and selfishness are
separated from the love of God: that they may be brought
out of the darkness into light.
O Lord, hear our prayer
And let our cry come unto thee.
Let us pray for all who mourn, and all who are lost in grief;
that they may find strength in the knowledge of thy eternal
purpose; for the depressed and the anxious, the lonely and the
doubting, and those in despair: that they may be led to the
certainty of thy love and find joy in human friendship.
O Lord, hear our prayer
And let our cry come unto thee.
Let us pray for the work of the united voluntary
organizations, and for God's continued blessing on this united
act of mercy.
O Lord, hear our prayer
And let our cry come unto thee.

And let us pray that Christians everywhere may be drawn into close unity with each other as they seek to obey the commands of Christ.

O Lord, hear our prayer

And let our cry come unto thee.

Liverpool Cathedral

319 A Prayer for Those Who Are, or Have Been in Prison

We pray first for those who are responsible for the maintenance of law and order in our community; for those who administer justice in the courts; and for those who are the victims of crime, violence and deceit.

Lord, hear us.

We pray for all prisoners, especially for those who are facing long sentences, and those who have lost faith in themselves and their fellow men, and have little hope for the future.

Lord, hear us.

We pray for young people; for those who have already come up against the law in juvenile and family courts; for those on probation and for those on the fringe of delinquency; and we pray for parents, teachers, youth leaders, clergy and all who try to help boys and girls to escape from the sordid and the second rate, and to find a true purpose in life.

Lord, hear us.

We pray for all those who have the custody and care of prisoners; for prison wardens, chaplains, officers; we pray for the Justice Department, and for those who direct the policy of all penile institutions.

Lord, hear us.

We pray for all those who have a special concern for the after-care of offenders: probation officers, and those who share with them the work of after-care, the wardens of hostels, and the employers of labour.

Lord, hear us.

We pray for those who have been released from prison; those who have managed to make good and those who continue to find the going hard; and we ask that we may

learn to be as forgiving of others as we trust God is forgiving
of us.

Lord, hear us.

We pray for ourselves as members of the community; and
we ask that our right respect for law and order may not
prevent our compassion and concern for those who have
failed to live up to the accepted standards of our society.

Lord, hear us.
Liverpool Cathedral

WORK

320 **Those Who Work at Holiday Times**

O God our Father, at this holiday season we pray for those
who must work in order to maintain the essential needs of
our country: for doctors and nurses; for the police; for those
who maintain the supply of gas and electricity to our houses;
for those who maintain public transport. We pray for those
and many others that Jesus Christ might draw near to them
and that they might not resent separation from their families
and friends, through Jesus Christ our Lord.   Amen.
Peter Markby

321 **Work**

Thank you, Lord, for the gift of work, and for the strength
in which to do it. Thank you for our brains and our senses,
and the strength in our limbs and bodies; help us to use them
well for you; to work well with other people; and to make
the place where we work a happier place. Help us to make the
work of others easier and more pleasant; and be with all who
find work difficult or dull or full of arguments. Bless those
for whom we work, and those who work for us; in the name
of Jesus, the carpenter, and the Saviour.   Amen.
Christopher Ilde

322   Starting a Job After Leaving School

O God our creator and preserver, who gives us the strength
to start new things; we ask you to guide and encourage those
who this year are leaving school and starting work; help them
to get used to new ways, new ideas, new people; give them
wisdom to know what is right and good, and the courage to
do it; and may they do their work knowing that it is for you,
and that you are with them; through Jesus Christ our Lord.
Amen.

Christopher Idle

323   Trades Unions and Their Leaders

God our Father, we thank you for the trades unions and for
all that they have achieved in the past to improve the wages
and conditions of workers. We ask you to bless all union
leaders that they may use the great powers they possess wisely
and well, and contribute to that justice in industrial relations
which is essential to their well being. And to all Christians
with positions of authority and responsibility in the unions
give your guidance that they may bring glory to your name;
through Jesus Christ our Lord.   Amen.

Peter Markby (adapted)

324   Industry

Almighty and everlasting God, we pray for all who work in
industry. Bless all meetings between employers and
employees. Remove all bitterness, distrust and prejudice from
their deliberations. Give to all a spirit of tolerance, and an
earnest desire to seek for justice and for truth; that all may
work together for the common good, through Jesus Christ
our Lord.   Amen.

W. A. Hampson

325   For the Unemployed

Bless, O Lord, all those who at the height of their powers
have been deprived of their jobs. Help them and their families

to adjust to this demand and deprivation, and enable them in their crisis to work together as a loving and courageous team. Grant that all who lose security of employment may find an inner security in Christ, and, always being active in his service, may be led to full employment once again. And to this end we pray that governments and industry may plan humanely and well, so that by serving God men may master their fate, through Jesus Christ our Lord.   Amen.
Dick Williams

326   For the Use and Understanding of Money

Help us and all people, dear Lord, to understand the purpose and place of money in our life. Keep before us the peril of loving it. Help us to make it our servant, and never our master. And let neither the lack of it, nor the possession of it, in any degree loosen our grasp upon reality, which is ours through love of Jesus Christ our Lord.   Amen.
Dick Williams

327   A Litany for Our Work

Let us remember that the first recorded command given to man was to work. Let us ask God's forgiveness for the times when we have considered our work as drudgery rather than as a gift from God.
Lord in mercy:
    Hear our prayer
Let us pray for all employers that they may carry out their responsibilities with justice and integrity. Let us pray for the members of this congregation who are employers.
Lord in mercy:
    Hear our prayer
Let us pray for all who are employed by others; that they might give good and honest work. Let us pray that Christians at work might seek above all to please God by their work.
Lord in mercy:
    Hear our prayer

Let us pray for the Trades Union movement; thanking God
for all that has been achieved in getting better working
conditions and fairer wages for workers. Let us pray for
trade union leaders and shop stewards that they may exercise
their great powers wisely and responsibly.
Lord in mercy:

Hear our prayer

Let us pray for those with whom we have relationships
through their work or through ours. Let us pray for our
colleagues at work. Let us pray for those who serve us week
by week and for our attitudes towards them – for the postman,
the milkman, the refuse collectors, for shop assistants and for
many others.
Lord, in mercy:

Hear our prayer

Let us pray for those whose work is dull and monotonous;
for those whose work is dangerous; for those whose work
causes them to be separated from their families for long periods;
and for those whose work brings them into situations where
they are greatly tempted.
Lord, in mercy:

Hear our prayer.

Let us pray for those who cannot work; for those who
cannot find employment; for those who cannot obtain work
because they are coloured immigrants; for those who are
disabled; and for those who have retired.
Lord, in mercy:

Hear our prayer.
Peter Markby

328　Professional Sport

We pray, Lord, for all engaged in professional sport as players,
administrators or businessmen. Help them to see their work as
part of a wider life, and help them to remember that all life
comes from you. May they set for themselves the highest
standards of personal and professional behaviour, both on the
field and off, and for those who follow their fortunes may they

provide an example to help make the heart of this great
nation sound; through Jesus Christ our Lord.   Amen.
Dick Williams

329   We pray, Father, for all who engage in sports and contests,
for their own pleasure and the entertainment of others,
especially in our own town (*or city*).
We pray that they may be kept from harm and injury. We ask
that through their knowledge of the laws of the game, they
may see that there are greater laws; that through their
experience of training and discipline they may see that there is
a nobler discipline; that through their desire for victory they
may be directed to the greatest triumph of all, and the goal
which is Christ, the Saviour of the world. For his name's
sake.   Amen.
Christopher Idle

330   Work

Let us think about our work in the presence of God.
Our jobs are varied:
Productive, unproductive;
Interesting, dull;
Satisfying, boring.
Some have good prospects, some are dead-end jobs.
We are thankful for automation, shorter hours, more money,
more leisure.
We place ourselves in the hands of God with our qualifications
and skills.
We also lift to him our employers and work-mates; all we
work with and for.
In his presence let us name our particular jobs.
(*All mention in turn their job and place of work.*)
We believe that God can use us in these jobs.
We believe that there are not good jobs and bad jobs, only
good workers and bad workers.
We thank God for the example of the men of faith of old:
David, shepherd.
Amos, farmer.

Peter, fisherman.
Paul, tentmaker.
Jesus, Carpenter.
Whatever your hand finds to do, do it with your might.[1]
Whatever your task, work heartily, as serving the Lord and
not men.[2]
Whether you are eating or drinking or whatever you are
doing do all in the name of the Lord Jesus.[3]
Simon H. Baynes

TRAVEL
331   Travellers

Lord Jesus Christ, you travelled once by hard and dangerous
roads; you drew near to your friends as they journeyed on
the way, both going along with them, and sharing with them
your truth; be present, we ask, with those who travel this
week (*especially those in our hearts this day*); guard them in every
danger; make them aware that you are with them; and bring
them safe and well to where they want to be; for your own
name's sake.   Amen.
Christopher Idle

332   Those Who Use the Roads

O God, who has taught us to love you, and to love our
neighbours as ourselves, give to us, and to all who use the
roads – to drive, to ride, or to walk – consideration and care
for all others; that death and injury may be caused to no one,
and that all who travel may go in safety, peace and joy;
through him who is the way, the truth and the life, Jesus
Christ our Lord.   Amen.
Frank M. Best

333   Road Safety

The roads have always been dangerous, Lord. It is only the
source of danger which varies. And now that the clatter of
hooves, the rumble of wooden wheels, and the shuffling feet

[1] Ecclesiastes 9.10 [2] Colossians 3.23 [3] 1 Corinthians 10.31.

of men are largely gone from our roads, so too have wild
beasts and highwaymen. Now is the day of the motor car:
its urgent urban scramble, its tiresome country roar. And we
have sadly learned that bandits never slew like this. Lord
protect our children; protect the strong; protect the elderly;
protect the nation. To those who design cars and build them,
to those who plan routes and build roads, give the highest
objectives they can devise for their work. And give us all,
those who drive and those who walk, the courtesy,
common sense and knowledge from which alone safety may
finally come; through Jesus Christ our Lord.   Amen.
W. N. Letheren

334   Air Travel

O God who has given to man the spirit and the powers which
express themselves in flight, bless all who are engaged in
travel by air:
bless aircraft designers, that in them knowledge and invention
may continually combine to produce aeroplanes which are
better and safer;
bless all who operate commercial airlines, that they may
faithfully put public safety before private profit;
bless all who devise routes and schedules, that they may make
constantly revised allowances for error;
bless those who coordinate departures and arrivals at busy
airports, that they may work with skill and sure judgment
within the safest limits;
bless all aircrews, that they may work with skill of mind,
strength of body, and peace of heart;
and bless all travellers, that they may be brought safely to
their journey's end;
through Jesus Christ our Lord.   Amen.
Dick Williams

SCIENCE AND SCIENTIFIC RESEARCH
335   The Peaceful Use of Science

For scientists who play the war game
With test-tubes of inventive hate

Creating, in their starched white coats,
Burgeoning masses of condensed pain
To tear life limb from limb.
Be Lord of their laboratories
And Master of their minds
And help them and those they serve to use their gifts
To further peace and love on earth:
Through Jesus Christ our Lord.   Amen.
based on a prayer by Susan Heywood

336   When man learned to fight with sticks
They soon became spears.
When he learned to fight with stones
They soon became bombs.
Now he flies the skies and sails the seas,
And all his armies march.
Lord help the leaders of mankind
To realize the power which science puts into their hands.
Help them to learn the ways of peace
Before hate and ignorance destroy our race:
Through Jesus Christ our Lord.   Amen.
based on a prayer by Susan Heywood

337   Scientists and Scientific Research

On starting a research project
God, show me truth and beauty through this work.
Give me honesty and courage to retrace my steps from each
blind alley.
Open my clouded understanding to the pattern behind the
tangled facts.
Rescue me at the end from unwarranted pride,
And grant that the insight you will give may not be misused
by me or others;
Through Jesus Christ our Lord.   Amen.
Eric Jenkins

338   Fellow Members of a Research Team

Thank you, God, for this research team.
We are so different in our skills and in ourselves –
The technician and the scholar,
The mathematician, and the intuitive thinker,
The washer-up and the brewer of tea.
Forgive us our lack of a deep concern for each other.
We do care about the truth,
And we are grateful when it dawns upon us.
Send it again, but send love too.
Perhaps our team will then see something of Christ.   Amen.
Eric Jenkins

339   A Team's Prayer About the Publication of Scientific Discoveries

God, we would like to be the first in print. Our names at the end of the letter in the 'Journal'.
We can almost see the solution to the puzzle.
Obvious, now we think of it.
But it means a new chapter in the textbooks.
A moment of truth came, and we thank you.
But the others—in Japan, Russia, Europe—have they seen it yet?
They will. Truth is for sharing. But by people, not by computers.
That is why we would like to be the first in print.
Nevertheless, your will be done. Amen.
Eric Jenkins

340   Space Travel and Research

O Lord our God, the heavens declare your glory, and the moon and the stars which you have ordained; yet you have given to men dominion over the world of your hands. We pray today for safety for those who travel far beyond the earth, that the skill and knowledge of scientists and explorers may be used for the benefit of all men, and the glory of your name.   Amen.
Christopher Idle

341   O God, the creator of the universe, and maker of the minds
of men; grant a safe return to the astronauts travelling in
space. Grant wisdom to all who make decisions concerning
the vast sums of money involved in such enterprises, that
they may reflect your will. And bring good out of all that is
happening today; for Jesus Christ's sake.   Amen.
Andrew Warner

342   O God, the creator of all: we thank you for the wisdom
which has set us in so fair a world, and for the same wisdom
which has set this world in so vast a universe. Help us to care
properly for this planet, and all the people who live upon it,
and also to respond intelligently to the mystery and
challenge of the wider creation. We thank you for the spirit
of enquiry and adventure which helps man to master his
environment, and pray for those now engaged in the
exploration of space: grant to them a motive which is right,
a will that is pure, and the blessings of safety and peace of
mind. And so govern the minds of men and nations, O Lord,
that the knowledge which is won may be used for the good of
all and the harm of none; through Jesus Christ our Lord.
Dick Williams

343   We thank you, Lord, for revealing to the eyes of searching
men still more of the wonders of creation. Teach us also how
to use the knowledge being won. Grant that success may not
breed presumption, and that courage may not lapse into
carelessness. Give to all who risk their lives and loved ones
the blessings of your peace and care, and may all who direct
and execute journeys into space grow also in the
knowledge of God their Saviour. And so guide the desire of
nations, O Lord, that the gigantic efforts being directed into
space research may bear fruits of peace in the affairs of men,
through Jesus Christ our Lord.   Amen.
Dick Williams

344   **Space Research**

Creator God, Lord of the Universe; we thank you for giving
to men the spirit of enquiry and adventure, and the power to

obey your commandment – to have dominion over creation.
Grant to those engaged in space research a motive that is
right, a will that is pure, and the blessing of your protection.
And so order the unruly wills of men that the knowledge
which they win may be used for the good of all and the harm
of none, through Jesus Christ our Lord.   Amen.
Dick Williams

345   A Right Use of Knowledge

We thank you, Lord, for this wonderful world with all its
resources, so many of which are recently discovered, so many
yet to be found. We thank you for the trained minds and
patient personalities which harness earth's powers to human
needs. We thank you for machines which give us more leisure;
for jet planes which make travel more simple and speedy; for
radio and television which bring people from the ends of the
earth into our homes; for research into the causes of disease,
and drugs that heal our minds and bodies; for space research
into unknown worlds. Accept our thanks, O Lord, and accept
too our penitence for the many ways we use our knowledge
for destruction instead of building up, for causing suffering
instead of happiness, despair instead of hope.
May your Holy Spirit invade the minds of people of all
nations – scientists, technologists, rulers and politicians – that
your gifts to us may be a blessing and not a curse, that men
may learn to live with each other in friendship and
understanding, for Christ's sake.   Amen.
author unknown (adapted)

ART AND ARTISTS
346   For Vision

O heavenly Father, who has filled the world with beauty;
open our eyes to behold your gracious hand everywhere, that
rejoicing in your creation we may learn to serve you with
gladness; for the sake of him through whom all things were
made, your Son Jesus Christ our Lord.   Amen.
Society of St Luke the Painter

347   **The Consecration of Art**

We thank you, O God, for all the wonders you have made,
for the creative gifts you have given to man. We offer our
thanks, in humility and gladness, for all who use these gifts to
increase the richness of life; for the consecration of art to
your service; and for all things that help us to see the true
nature of your creation, through Jesus Christ our Lord.
Amen.
Society of St Luke the Painter

348   **Penitence for Poor Art**

Almighty God, author of all beauty and goodness, forgive us
and all men for the misuse of your many gifts, both now and
in the past, through selfishness and ignorance. Forgive our
failure to exercise a proper care for these gifts by offering you
things that are unworthy. Pardon our sins and let your
forgiveness open our eyes to new opportunities of service and
a new awareness of your glory; for the sake of Jesus Christ
our Saviour.   Amen.
Society of St Luke the Painter

349   **Artists and Craftsmen**

O God, whose spirit in our hearts teaches us to desire your
perfection, to seek for truth and to rejoice in beauty:
enlighten and inspire all artists and craftsmen in whatever is
true, pure and lovely, that your name may be honoured and
your will done on earth; for Jesus' sake.   Amen.
Society of St Luke the Painter

350   **Christian Art Organizations**

Almighty Father, may the Holy Spirit guide all Christian
groups concerned with the improvement of art, that in
closer cooperation their aims may be more fully realized
through Jesus Christ our Lord.   Amen.
Society of St Luke the Painter

351   Those Deprived of Beauty

Dear Father God, whose blessed Son Jesus Christ showed
compassion to those deprived of your good gifts: help us to
enrich the lives of those starved of the enjoyment of beauty,
that through our efforts the wonders of your creation may be
known more and more by all your children; through the same
Jesus Christ our Lord.   Amen.
Society of St Luke the Painter

352   A Painter's Prayer

Loving Father, source of order and form in life: inspire us in
our work that we may constantly seek your guidance,
acknowledge your presence, and daily strive to serve you
faithfully; for Jesus' sake.   Amen.
Society of St Luke the Painter

353   Artists

We thank you, God of creation, for the faculties by which we
may perceive beauty, and the heart with which to love it.
Give us eyes to see and ears to hear each sight and sound
which tells your love for man. And since you are greater than
the works of your own hands, let us not be content to love
your world without much more loving you, forever beyond
and above it as you are, inconceivably greater and more
glorious than all our senses can record; through Jesus Christ
our Lord.   Amen.
Dick Williams

354   An Artist's Prayer

O God, our Father, who clothes the world in beauty, look
down we beseech you with mercy upon all artists. Open our
eyes that we may see with true vision; quicken our minds;
guide our hands to interpret the beauty of your creation and
inspire us to convey your message to the world; through Jesus
Christ our Lord.   Amen.
Elsie Blakey

MUSIC AND MUSICIANS
355   Thanksgiving for Music

Father, we thank you for the many ways we can express
ourselves, but above all for the gift of music. We thank you
for the way it can describe every emotion: joy and delight;
melancholy and sadness; wonder and worship; love and
devotion. We thank you that music can soothe the soul and
bring solace to those who mourn. And we thank you, too,
that like the Israelites of old, we can make merry before you
and show our joy in music and song, singing and making
melody in our heart, through Jesus Christ our Lord.   Amen.
Patricia Mitchell

356   Musicians

O Lord Jesus Christ, whose birth was heralded by angels'
song, and whose death for sinners is extolled by the music of
heaven; grant that those who use voices and instruments to
show your glory may also display in their lives that harmony
which echoes your praise; for your own name's sake.   Amen.
Christopher Idle

357   Composers

Bless all those, O Lord, who compose music: those who take
the sounds of the earth, the passions of the heart, and the
motions of the mind and bind all together in the mystery of
music. May their greatest love be for you, O God; their
greatest delight your praise; their greatest reward the vision
of yourself; their greatest work a part of the music of heaven,
through Jesus Christ our Lord.   Amen.
Dick Williams

MASS MEDIA
358   Entertainers

O God, grant to all whose work is to give joy and happiness
to others the reminder that their gifts come from you. Help
them not to forget, as they offer these before the

footlights, that God's Son, Jesus Christ, came to be the
brightest of lights, the one that brought joy to the whole
world.   Amen.
C. Edwyn Young

359   Thinkers and Writers

O God, the inventor of thought, the creator of speech, bless
all those who work with thoughts and words and ideas: grant
that their minds might grow upward into light; enter into
their thinking as redeemer, inspiration and Lord; so may the
thinkers and writers of the world become the spokesmen of
divinity and the servants of mankind, through Jesus Christ,
the eternal Word.   Amen.
Dick Williams

360   Novelists, and Others

For human hearts and minds we thank you, Lord, and pray
for those who tell the stories of their interplay. We ask you to
bless all novelists, dramatists, poets and journalists, and pray
that they may love their creator more than their own
creations, and worship the one who made them more than
the things they make, so that saved from idolatry, they may
find new dimensions for their minds, new powers for their
pens, and new worlds for men's desires, through Jesus Christ,
the Lord of man's story, and the end to which it moves.
Amen.
Dick Williams

361   The Mass Media

O God, whose blessed Son Jesus Christ is the eternal Word,
in whom may be read the good news of creation, grant to all
who speak or write what many hear or read that love of truth
which leads to love of God, and that love of God which makes
communication of thought a good and holy thing; through
Jesus Christ our Lord.   Amen.
Dick Williams

362   Discrimination in Reading

O God, there seems so much to read, yet so little time to read
it. Inspire our judgment of what books to read, what magazines
and papers to take. Give us wisdom to skip well, and not to
waste our time on trivialities, so that all the thoughts we take
in through the printed page may be to the increase of our own
maturity, and so to the ultimate advancement of your kingdom;
through Jesus Christ our Lord.   Amen.
Andrew Warner

MARRIAGE AND FAMILY LIFE
363   Engaged Couples

Thank you, Lord Jesus Christ, for enriching the wedding at
Cana in Galilee, both by your presence and by your
generous gifts; please also enrich those (*known to us in this
church*) who are engaged to be married.
Grant that no couple may be joined together unequally or
wrongly; and grant that those whom you are calling to be
married may grow in honesty, maturity, and love for each
other; and that their married lives may draw their strength
and unity from you, and reflect your glory to others.   Amen.
Christopher Idle

364   Penitence and Thanks By Married Couples

Lord, we are sorry and we ask your forgiveness
That sometimes we show lack of respect, and understanding
and love;
That we neglect each other by neglecting to pray for each
other;
That we have often spoiled the perfect relationship you planned
for us;
And yet we also want to thank you
For the happiness we have known together
For the sadness we have faced together
For the problems we are overcoming together

For the love which you give us which is completely
unspoiled.
In the name of Jesus Christ, our Lord.
Christopher Idle

365   Newlyweds

O God, who in your Word has compared marriage to the
perfect union between Jesus your Son and the Church his
bride; be present we pray with all those newly married, as they
set up a new home together;
Grant them lasting faithfulness to you and to each other; true
unity with you and with each other; increasing love for you
and for each other;
That they may know that unless the Lord builds the house,
the builders' work is all in vain;
And that you will make their homes places where others may
meet with yourself; through Jesus Christ our Lord.
Christopher Idle

366   At the Time of an Engagement

Lord we thank you for the gift of love; the love of God for
man, and man for God.
We thank you for human love, that of man for woman and
woman for man.
We ask that during the months of engagement you will guide
us in all our ways, in our relationship to each other and in
our preparations for the marriage, so that on our wedding
day we may give our whole minds to the joy of the service
and the gathering together of those we love; through Jesus
Christ our Lord.   Amen.
Kenneth Thornton

367   For Use After the Calling of Banns

We ask your blessing, O Lord, on the couples whose banns
have been called today. During the last weeks before the
wedding, when there is so much to occupy their time, grant
them a deepening conviction of their love for each other, and

your call on their lives. Grant them joy on their wedding day
and your happiness in their future together; through Jesus
Christ, whose presence brought such joy at Cana.   Amen.
Kenneth Thornton

368   Wedding Day

We thank you for the dawning of this day and for your love
renewed and shown every morning. We pray for those who
are to be married today and ask that you will give them great
joy in the anticipation of the fulfilment of their love. For their
parents we ask your nearness; for them a great consciousness
of belonging to each other; and for all who are called to
marriage a faithfulness to their promises, through Jesus Christ
our Lord.   Amen.
Kenneth Thornton

369   A Baby in the Family

O God our Father, we marvel that you created the world and
all that is in it. The news of our child fills us with wonder
that you ask us to be part of your plan. Help us to contain
our joy in the confirmation of our hopes. We pray for our
child even now. Prepare our lives and our home so that we
may show this child your love from the first day of its birth.
We thank you in Jesus' name.   Amen.
Kenneth Thornton

370   On the Arrival of a Baby

Thank you Lord for the safe arrival of our child, and for the
care of doctors and nurses. We thank you for the gift of life
and we ask that this child may enjoy a happy time in youth
and a useful life of service; through Jesus Christ our Lord,
who himself grew in wisdom and stature as well as in favour
with God and men.   Amen.
Kenneth Thornton

371   A Prayer for a Child on its First Day at School

Lord we thank you for this home. It is rather like a harbour,
where safety and peace are to be found. In our first adventures
alone make us brave and true. Help us in our lessons, may we
find good friends and enjoy our new adventures; through
Jesus, who goes with us.   Amen.
Kenneth Thornton

372   A Child's Prayer at Night

Lord Jesus Christ,
In your arms tonight,
Help us to sleep
With our eyes shut tight.
Help us this and every day
To be deaf to Satan
And to hear what you say.   Amen.
Alison Williams

373   A Child's Prayer in the Morning

Dear Lord, may the love that is hidden in us be shown to
others: to people we dislike, to ones who are not as lucky as
ourselves. May we not be deaf to your voice; help us to
understand you; help us to do what you say.   Amen.
Alison Williams

374   When Tragedy Hits the Home

We never imagined what this day would bring. It started off
in anticipation of the happy routine of life. The day has
grown dark with sadness. You usually give us joy but now you
have asked us to take pain and heartache. Help us to bear our
sorrows, and may we know the comradeship of Jesus Christ,
the sorrow-bearer.   Amen.
Kenneth Thornton

375   On the First Signs of Tension in the Marriage

Lord Jesus Christ you know that when we make promises we
intend to keep them, and yet we so often fail. You know that
small differences of opinion soon become great rifts. We are
often not humble enough to be honest with each other and
soon there is a barrier between us. Give us your courage to
share our failures, our unfaithfulness and our difficulties so
that we may become perfectly one, as you are one with the
Father.   Amen.
Kenneth Thornton

376   Re-marriage of a Divorced Partner

We know, O God, that you are everywhere.
We thank you that as we exchanged promises today you were
listening.
Grant us now your blessing.
The blessing of a Father who cares and watches over us
understandingly,
The blessing of the Son who taught us how to live faithfully
and perseveringly,
The blessing of your Holy Spirit who binds us together in
heart and home.   Amen.
Kenneth Thornton

377   Homemaker's Prayer for Contentment

Dear Lord, help us to be happy doing the work you give us
to do, even if it is often monotonous. When the babies need
to be fed, meals to be cooked, and there is an everlasting war
to be waged with the rising tide of toys and books and
papers: give us the good sense to take time to stop and think
of you and of your goodness, because this is the only way to
peace and contentment; through Jesus Christ our Lord.
Amen.
Marjorie Hampson

378   Homemaker's Thanksgiving

Thank you, Lord, for our homes and families; thank you for
our health and happiness; thank you for the good times and
for helping us to cope with the times that are not so good.
Thank you for your love and for life itself.   Amen.
Marjorie Hampson

379   Thanksgiving for Marriage

*(Everyone stands and a husband and wife lead an Act of
Thanksgiving for Marriage. The people make their reply loudly and
with enthusiasm.)*
Let us thank God for our wedding day.
> *Thanks be to God.*

Let us thank God for the wonder of falling in love and
making love.
> *Thanks be to God.*

(Husband:)   Let us thank God for our wives.
(Husbands:)   *Thanks be to God.*
(Wife:)   Let us thank God for our husbands.
(Wives:)   *Thanks be to God.*
Let us thank God for our homes.
> *Thanks be to God.*

Let us thank God for our children.
> *Thanks be to God.*

Let us thank God for our friends.
> *Thanks be to God.*

Let us thank God for everything.
> *Thanks be to God.*

*from the Service 'In Praise of Marriage' conducted in Liverpool
Cathedral*

380   A Reaffirmation of Marriage Vows

*(A husband and wife lead the congregation in the reaffirmation of
their marriage vows. First, while everyone sits, they read from the
New Testament.)*
(Husband:)   Listen to what St Paul has to say about
marriage, and how he sees in it a mirror of Christ's love for
his Church.

(*Wife:*) 'Husbands, love your wives, as Christ also loved the Church and gave himself up for it, to consecrate it, cleansing it by water and word, so that he might present the Church to himself all glorious, with no stain or wrinkle or anything of the sort, but holy and without blemish.'

(*Husband:*) 'In the same way, men also are bound to love their wives, as they love their own bodies. In loving his wife a man loves himself. For no one ever hated his own body; on the contrary he provides and cares for it; and that is how Christ treats the Church, because it is his Body, of which we are living parts.'

(*Wife:*) Thus it is that (in the words of Scripture): 'A man shall leave his father and mother and shall be joined to his wife, and the two shall become a single body'. It is a great truth that is hidden here.

(*Husband:*) 'I for my part refer it to Christ and to the Church, but it applies also individually: each of you must love his wife as his very self;'

(*Wife:*) 'And the woman must see to it that she pays her husband all respect.'

(*Everyone stands for the Reaffirmation of the Marriage Vows.*)

(*Husband:*) I call upon the husbands here to reaffirm their marriage vows, saying with me:

(*Husbands:*) I reaffirm my solemn promise to my wife to have and to hold, for better, for worse; for richer, for poorer; in sickness and in health; to love and to cherish, till death us do part.

(*Wife:*) I call upon the wives here to reaffirm their marriage vows to their husbands.

(*Wives:*) I reaffirm my promise to my husband to have and to hold, for better for worse; for richer for poorer; in sickness and in health; to love and to cherish, till death us do part.

Liverpool Cathedral

381 Family Life

Father, we praise you that in your great wisdom you have planned for us a life in which all our deep desires can be met. We thank you for one another, and for all the gifts which

make us one, and especially for the unique relationship
between man and woman.

We praise you that we were born as babies into family life, and
that for parents and children there is a twofold blessing. We
thank you that as each family grows and branches out, so
brothers and sisters, grandparents and grandchildren too, all
have a part to play in the life of each member.

Above all Father, we thank and praise you that we can be one
with you, through Jesus Christ our Lord.   Amen.

Patricia Mitchell

382   Family Life and Fellowship

Father, we thank you that you have seen fit to establish us in
families, so that we may live together, play together, work
together, rejoice together, and grieve together. But above all
we thank you that we are able to be members of your family
the church; that through your Son Jesus Christ we are able to
become your children.

We thank you that no matter how widely spread throughout
the world our Christian family may be, our hearts may be
united in prayer so that we are able to share one another's
burdens, rejoice in one another's blessings and strengthen one
another in the power of your Holy Spirit.

And we thank you that in your wisdom you have set aside a
day when we can gather together for praise and worship and,
drawn aside from everyday living, be renewed together as a
family by your Holy Spirit, through Jesus Christ our Lord.
Amen.

Patricia Mitchell

383   Thanksgiving for Children

Dear Father, we give you thanks for children, and particularly
for those who are committed to our care. We thank you for
their innocence, their laughter, their loving and their
unquestioning trust in us. Father, help us to give them,
through teaching and the example of our own lives, a simple

and steadfast faith, a loving heart and a cheerful nature, that
they may be equipped to be citizens not only of this world but
also of the next, through Jesus Christ our Lord.   Amen.
Patricia Mitchell

384   Broken Homes

O Lord our heavenly Father, look mercifully upon those
whose lives have been shattered by the breaking up of their
homes. Grant to your children freedom from resentment, and
the strength to seek your will in every situation. Prosper, we
pray, all work of reconciliation, that all may come to
acknowledge you, the only perfect Father, who with the Son
and the Holy Spirit, lives and reigns for ever and ever.
Amen.
Andrew Warner

385   Marriages Under Stress

O Lord God, we thank you for the gift of marriage, that gift
which leads to the height of shared joy or to the depths of
shared bitterness. We pray for those who have suffered hurt
in marriage; for those who have inflicted it, and for those
whose greatest unhappiness stems from the closeness of their
partner.
O Lord, who in love created the complexities of the human
mind, and in power conquered the evil that invades it: bring
wholeness to those who are in fragments and unity to those
who long for it, that we may all finally be united with yourself
and with one another.   Amen.
Susan Williams

386   The Divorced

O Lord, we pray for all those who, full of confidence and love,
once chose a partner for life, and are now alone after final
separation. May they all receive the gift of time, so that hurt
and bitterness may be redeemed by healing and love, personal
weakness by your strength, inner despair by the joy of knowing
you and serving others, through Jesus Christ our Lord.
Amen.
Susan Williams

387 Family Planning

O Lord our heavenly Father, who has given to your children
both the joy of sharing in the work of your creation and the
responsibility of controlling it: grant that married couples may
make right use of the ways you have provided for planning their
families. Guide those who provide them with medical and
social guidance, that there may be true reverence for life,
through him by whom all things were made, your only
begotten Son Jesus Christ. Amen.
Andrew Warner (adapted)

388 For Understanding

Father of Jesus, give grace and understanding to all who live
in families. May the spirit of peace settle between parent and
child, brother and sister. May the young realize that the old
may be wiser than they. May the old see how many of the
young are trying to set up your kingdom on earth. And by
their harmony may they give glory to you, O Father, and to
the Son, through the one Spirit, blest forever. Amen.
P. D. Reynolds (adapted)

389 For Those Preparing to Bring Their Children to Baptism

O God our Father, from whom every family in heaven and
on earth takes it name: please be present to bless the families
of the children soon to be baptized as members of your
Church. Help the parents and God-parents to see the meaning
of your saving Gospel; to make their promises sincerely and
heartily; to pray for their children; and to teach them of holy
things; so that they may all share in your gift of eternal life,
now and for ever. In the name of Jesus Christ our Lord.
Amen.
Christopher Idle

390 For Those Recently Baptized

Lord Jesus Christ, because you welcomed the little ones who
were brought to you, we pray for those who were this

(*morning/afternoon/evening*) added to the fellowship of your
church.
Guard them in health and strength as they grow up; help
their parents to trust you and to make each home your dwelling;
and use the children's work of this church to nourish their
faith in you; for the glory of your saving name.   Amen.
Christopher Idle

391   Children and Children's Children

O Father and maker of all things, we are the work of your
hands. Continue your work in us, that we may show forth
your righteousness to our children and our children's
children; for the love of your blessed Son, our Saviour Jesus
Christ.   Amen.
Margaret Girdlestone

392   For Children Who Lose Their Parents

Almighty God, we thank you for teaching us through Jesus
that all the power of the universe is focused upon us in
fatherly care; and in this faith we commend to your loving
kindness all children who have lost their parents.
Give special inspiration and grace to those who look after
them in the early moments of their bereavement. Give great
love and joy to those who care for them over the following
years. And in and through their bereavement help the children
to trust you as their heavenly father, knowing that their
earthly parents are in your care, and that those who care for
them are sent by you to take their place.
So may they love and serve you all their days and joyfully care
for children in their turn; through Jesus Christ our Lord.
Amen.
Dick Williams

393   A Sick Child

Our helplessness, our sorrow, our fear, and our anxiety are all
profoundly known to you, O Lord, and so too is our love, our
hope, our desire, our prayer, our faith.
We believe that you love our precious child more than we do

ourselves, we believe that you made (*him*) and cherish (*him*)
and have given to (*him*) a place in your purposes. And so we
believe that nothing can happen which is outside the range of
your love and power.
Grant to (*him*) health, and life, we pray. But since (*he*) is your
child more than (*he*) is ours, and since you see what lies
beyond our own horizons help us also to say 'Your will be
done'; knowing that your will is *(his)* peace and ours, through
Jesus Christ our Lord.   Amen.
Dick Williams

YOUNG PEOPLE: SCHOOLS AND COLLEGES
394   Young People of the Church

O God our Father, bless we pray the young people of our
Church; keep them faithful to you when the world beckons
in the opposite direction; guide them in the great decisions
they have to take concerning a career and choice of marriage
partner; and grant that in you they may find true peace, so
that armed with your Spirit they may do great things for you,
for the sake of Jesus Christ our Lord.   Amen.
Andrew Warner

395   Young Disciples

O God our Father, we praise you for those who have put
their trust in Jesus Christ as their Lord and Saviour at camps,
retreats, rallies, or conferences, in this church or at their
homes. May their faith grow, may their love increase, and
may they find encouragement and fellowship within the
church. Help us, we pray, to give to all who have become your
disciples the support of our friendship and our prayers,
through Jesus Christ our Lord. Amen.
Peter Markby

396   Children Leaving Primary School

O Lord our heavenly Father, bless all who are leaving this
school this term; watch over them every day of their life;
protect them in danger; help them in difficulty; and encourage
them in all they do in your service.

Keep them faithful in their prayers, loyal in their friendships, and happy in their new schools, and help them to know that although they are leaving some of their friends that they will be making new ones. Help them to remember that you are always near, their Saviour and friend, who lives and reigns with the Father and the Holy Spirit, one God, for ever and ever. Amen.
Andrew Warner

397 For Those With Exams Soon

We remember before you, O God of truth, all those students and scholars facing examinations this (*week/month*); especially those known to us, and those who know you. Grant that they may readily remember all that they have honestly learned, and give a true account of their ability; so that whatever may depend upon the results, they may willingly give their future to your disposing. Through Jesus Christ our Lord.
Christopher Idle

398 For a School

Father, we hold before you now in prayer our life together in this school.
Help us to give to it of our best, and to receive in turn the best it has to give.
Teach us to know the joys of discovery, the warmth of friendship, the satisfaction of attempting and achieving, and the demands of truth.
Open for us week by week new windows on our world; increase our understanding of ourselves and others.
May teachers and taught alike seek first your Kingdom, to the good of this school and the glory of your Name; through Jesus Christ our Lord. Amen.
Timothy Dudley-Smith

399 A Teacher's Prayer

When the class is trying and the progress slow;
When our duties are irksome and the time long;

When our patience is exhausted and we have no reserve;
Good Lord, help us.
From staffroom gossip which profits nothing;
From the sarcastic word which is meant to sting;
From lack of patience and loss of temper:
Good Lord, save us.
A word of encouragement for the cheerful plodder;
A word of timely warning for the careless and idle;
An even disposition which refuses to be ruffled:
Good Lord, give us.
K. A. Clegg

400   A Pupil's Prayer

That which is worth knowing
That which is worth hearing
That which is worth seeing
That which is worth believing
Give us grace to find.
Give us this day our daily bread.
May I work hard as one who needs not be ashamed.
Even today may I learn something which interests and excites
me.
Even today may I discipline myself to be careful and
thorough.
Even today may I exert myself to the utmost of my ability.
Even today may I learn to seek after knowledge and truth.
Today and every day.
K. A. Clegg

401   Teacher and Learner

May we explore together the territory of knowledge.
May we learn together the mysteries of truth.
May we share together the experience of beauty.
May we join together in the joy of physical activity.
May we ever remember that you, the author of all knowledge,
yourself Goodness, Truth and Beauty, delight to share all
experience with us.

A time for working; a time for playing.
A time for laughter; a time for gravity.
A time for words; a time for silence.
A time for business; a time for rest.
A time for questioning; a time for listening.
A time for prayer; a time for action.
Lord, all our time is in your hands; help us to use it well.

As the time for examinations draws near we need your help.
Help us to work hard, using all the powers of mind you have given us.
Help us to understand the things we are taught, and give wisdom to our teachers.
Help us to persevere, making every effort to overcome our difficulties.
Help us to enjoy our limited leisure time to the full.
Help us not to be anxious but to trust your over-all concern for us.
And to your name be all the glory, thanksgiving and praise today and every day.
K. A. Clegg

402   The Day of the Examination

Lord, we need your help.
We need a calm mind; grant us your peace.
We need a clear head; grant us your wisdom.
We need to be careful; grant us your patience.
We need to be inspired: grant us your enthusiasm.
Keep us from all panic as we put our trust in your power to keep us this day.
K. A. Clegg

403   For Our School

We thank you, Lord, for this school to which we belong; for its foundation and continuing life under your directing power; for all who work in it and for it.
Thank you for the service given by teachers and pupils; by domestic and kitchen staff; by clerical staff and those who govern its business, and by parents and friends; may all these work together for its common purpose.

We pray that individual gifts and talents may be discovered,
developed and used for you and for the good of others;
Through him who as a man both learned with care and
taught with power, Jesus Christ our Saviour.
Christopher Idle

404   Across the Generation Gap

In order to understand the problems of young people, O
Lord, help us to remember our own youth, and out of that
memory to consider:
The insecurity of the world in which young people live today;
The talk of war and the practice of it;
The affluence of so much of society and the encouragement it
gives them to possess and not to give;
The unbelief in spiritual things among many who shape their
education;
The strain of examinations;
The propaganda of many kinds to which they are subjected:
All these things are stumbling blocks which our own generation
have erected for them.
So we thank you, Lord, for the vision and courage of so many
young people today; for their hatred of hypocrisy and their
search for the truth.
Help us and our generation to have wisdom and an
understanding heart. May we so live that young people may
want to discover things of beauty and goodness, and may
come to know the truth in Jesus Christ, their Lord and ours,
for we ask it in his name.   Amen.
adapted from a prayer by an unknown author

405   A Litany for the Young

Let us give thanks for Christ's revelation to us of God's love
for children and of their infinite value in his sight.
> *We thank you O Lord.*
For his tender compassion towards them; for his burning
indignation against those who do them wrong; for his deep
and overflowing love, drawing them with irresistible attraction

to himself; for his message of their nearness to the Father of
all;

We thank you O Lord.

For the beauty of children and their joy in all beautiful things,
for their mirth and laughter, and for the joy and light they
bring into the world;

We thank you O Lord.

For their enthusiasm, their abounding energy, and their love
of the heroic and adventurous; for their candid, generous
trust in those around them, and for their quick response to
calls of love and service;

We thank you O Lord.

O Lord forgive because there are still children in need of
care and love.

O Lord forgive.

Because homes are broken by selfishness, pride and greed,

O Lord forgive.

Because even in our affluence, children remain in spiritual and
moral danger,

O Lord forgive.

Because children continue to be exploited by the greedy and
the lustful,

O Lord forgive.

Because children in many parts of the world suffer from
disease and malnutrition,

O Lord forgive.

Because many children are homeless and many are not taught
to read or write,

O Lord forgive.

Because many children live in fear, and have not heard the
good news of Jesus Christ,

O Lord forgive

Because these great needs cannot always be met for want of
skilled workers and adequate resources,

O Lord forgive.

Let us all say together this prayer:

O Lord God, Forgive what we have been, Sanctify what we are,
Direct what we shall be; for Jesus Christ's sake.   Amen.

Liverpool Cathedral

406   A Children's Litany

For calling us into your great family of love: for making us
your sons and daughters; for putting your Spirit into our
hearts; for helping us to grow up into Christ:

O God, we thank and praise you.

For signing us with the sign of the Cross; for calling us to be
your faithful soldiers and servants; for giving us a cause to
fight for; for equipping us for your holy warfare:

O God, we thank and praise you.

For knowing our abilities and powers; for calling us to work
together; for giving us strength through fellowship; for
making us united in your service:

O God, we thank and praise you.

Help us to know you more and more; help us to know the
Bible and to love it; teach us how to talk to you and how to
listen to you; teach us to pray:

In your mercy, hear our prayer.

Help us to see the needs of other people; help us to want to
help; teach us how to do good; make us more and more
practical day by day:

In your mercy, hear our prayer.

Help us to see and know your will for our lives; show us
what you want us to become; lead us into the jobs and hobbies
and friendships which will please you and fulfil our being:

In your mercy, hear our prayer.

Bless our church, its Sunday school, its day school, its Scouts
and Guides and Cub Scouts and Brownies and its youth
clubs:

O Lord bless us all.

Bless all the babies who are baptized in this church, and bless
their mothers and fathers and godparents. Help us to help the
babies to grow up as true Christians, full members of the
church and true servants of mankind:

O Lord bless us all.

Comfort those who are sick or sad, make them brave in their
suffering, and bring them safely out of all their trouble:

In your mercy, hear our prayer.

Bless all the peoples of the world, and bring them to know

and love you through Jesus Christ our Lord, and grant that
from this knowledge they may arrange their lives and
organize the world in righteousness and peace:

In your mercy, hear our prayer.
Dick Williams

FRIENDS, FAMILY AND HOME
407   Friends

Remember O Lord today for good all our friends, for whom
we thank you; thank you for those who come to see us, or
who write to us, or who are always at hand to help us.
We ask you to bless them all today; some at home; some far
away; some who are travelling; some who are ill; some who
are sad.
Bless those, too, whom we find it hard to be friends with;
and make us true friends to one another and to the Lord
Jesus Christ, the friend of sinners. We ask this in his name.
Amen.
Christopher Idle

408   Friends and Neighbours

Heavenly Father, look in love on all our friends and
neighbours. Keep them from all harm, deepen our friendship
with them, and may we all grow in love of you, our Saviour
and friend, through Jesus Christ our Lord.   Amen.
M. H. Botting's collection

409   Absent Friends

O sweet and loving Lord Christ, our unseen yet eternal friend,
the giver of all true friendship and the guardian of our love,
we pray for all our friends and loved ones wherever in your
great world they may be.
Bless them with the fullness of your grace and power, and fill
their hearts and lives with yourself.
You alone know how much we love each other, and the pain
and loneliness of being separated. As we link our hands in
yours grant us to know the strength and peace of your

presence, and the sheltering warmth and comfort of your love, and keep us, O Lord, so near to yourself that we may evermore be near to each other, and, if it is your will, give us the renewal of our fellowship on earth and at last our perfect union in the friendship of our Father's home.   Amen.
Harold E. Evans

410   Holidays

O God our Father, we thank you for the times of rest from the normal daily round. We pray that those who are on holiday at this time may be enabled to find the threefold recreation of body, mind and spirit that will strengthen them for your service in the days that lie ahead; through Jesus Christ our Lord.   Amen.
Bernard Woolf

411   Those on Holiday

We thank you our Father that your purpose for men is that our lives should consist of work and recreation, of activity and rest, of business and holiday.
We pray for those who are now enjoying the opportunity of holidays. Enable them, we pray, to be refreshed in mind, body, and spirit, so that in the coming months they may be able to work more effectively and to serve you more faithfully, through Jesus Christ our Lord.   Amen.
Peter Markby

412   Holidays and Leisure

Heavenly Father, because you rested from your work of creation we thank you for the opportunities we have of holidays and leisure. Refresh our bodies, minds and souls so that we may return to our daily work better able to serve you, through Jesus Christ our Lord.   Amen.
M. H. Botting's collection

413   Marriage

O God our Father, you made men and women to live together in families: We pray that marriage may be held in honour;

that husbands and wives may live faithfully together; and that
members of every family may grow in mutual understanding,
love and courtesy; through Jesus Christ our Lord.   Amen.
M. H. Botting's collection

414   For Parents

Father, grant to all parents wisdom and understanding in the
upbringing of their children: that as they grow in stature so
too they may learn to love you more day by day, through
Jesus Christ.   Amen.
Joyce Francis

415   For Family Harmony

Forgive us, Lord, when jealousy, greed, temper, pride, or
indignation disturb the peace of our family. Help us to find
the right words and the right actions to soothe and heal the
hurt. Forgive us when we quarrel. Help us to forgive others:
help others to forgive us; through Jesus Christ our Lord.
Amen.
Patricia Mitchell

416   Heavenly Father, we thank you for our homes and families,
for our food and clothing, and for all the happiness that
parents and children can share. We ask that your love may
surround us, your care protect us and that we may know
your peace at all times, for Jesus' sake.   Amen.
M. H. Botting's collection

417   Our Homes

Be with us, Lord, where people see us at our best and at our
worst. Make our homes places where we can speak of God
without hypocrisy and serve our loved ones without self-
interest; through Jesus Christ our Lord.
Ian D. Bunting

FAMILY PRAYERS

418   For the Home

O God, whose Son Jesus Christ prepared to save the world
by serving in a home: help us as a family to love and serve
you and one another. Give us those blessings which will
enable us to make this dwelling a worthy place for your
presence; through Jesus Christ our Lord.   Amen.
F. W. Street

419   **Absent Members of the Family**

Loving Father, you are present everywhere and care for all
your children: we commend to you the member(*s*) of this
family now parted from us. Watch over (*him*), protect and
guide (*him*). Surround (*him*) and us with your love, and bring
us all to that home of many mansions where partings are no
more; through Jesus Christ our Lord.   Amen.
F. W. Street

420   **Thanksgiving**

Almighty God, the protector of all who trust in you, we thank
you for your goodness to us during the past day: for work to
do, and health and strength to do it; for our home and the
love which binds us together with you and one another; for
protection from harm and danger, and for sins forgiven.
Receive our thanks for the sake of Jesus Christ our Lord.
Amen.
F. W. Street

421   **Protection**

O God, our Father, keep us your children safe under your
protection this day. May we feel the strength of your Spirit
within us, the warmth of your love around us, and your
presence through all our way. Let no danger daunt us, no
temptation master us, nor any evil thing separate us from
yourself, Hear us, O Father, for your dear Son's sake.   Amen.
Harold E. Evans

422   Inspiration

Fill us, O Lord, with the Holy Spirit, that we may go forth
with eagerness and joy to love and serve you in holiness, and
to do your perfect will, through Jesus Christ our Lord. Amen.
Harold E. Evans

423   This Week

We thank you, heavenly Father, for all the opportunities
which will be ours during this week. We thank you for the
people who will serve us in the shop and office and classroom.
We thank you for those who make our lives brighter – the
postman and the friendly neighbour. We thank you for those
who make our lives easier – the dustman and the policeman.
As people do so much for us, help us not to make their work
a burden but rather look for ways in which we may help
others too; for Jesus Christ's sake.   Amen.
Ian D. Bunting

424

We thank you, Lord, that we can freely worship you. Help us,
we pray, to continue our worship through the coming week
by living lives which are filled with love, both for you and for
all mankind.   Amen.

425   For the Week

We give you thanks, O God our Father,
For every good and perfect gift;
For our work on Monday;
For our games on Saturday;
For our worship on Sunday;
And for our Saviour Jesus Christ who is with us all through
the week.   Amen.
Christopher Idle

426   Morning

O Lord, enable us this day to reveal your glory in all we
think, and say, and do; that your presence may bless and

strengthen us all the day long, through Jesus Christ our Lord.
Amen.
Michael Saward

427   Thank you Father for a quiet night. Help us in the new day
that stretches before us. We do not know what it will
contain; it is unknown. We only know ourselves, and the
problems and possibilities of our character.
Help us to be friendly and kind to one another, and to others
whom we shall meet. Help us to curb our impatience and the
unkind words which may come to our lips. And if we have to
face danger or make decisions which are difficult, give us
courage to do what we know to be right. Help us to look for
opportunities of service wherever we may be, and help us to
remember that everything we do can be offered to you as an
act of worship. So may we not be ashamed when this day is
over, for Christ's sake.   Amen.
based on a prayer by an unknown author

428   Saturday Evening

Come to us, Lord Jesus, when we receive the bread of life and
the cup of salvation. Cleanse our hearts from sin that they may
be worthy of so great a guest.   Amen.
F. W. Street

429   Before Bible Reading

O God, speak to us through your Word. Pour out upon us
your grace that we may learn your will and obey your call;
through Jesus Christ our Lord.   Amen.
F. W. Street

430   A Grace

For these gifts of food, and for your care day by day, O
heavenly Father, we thank you.   Amen.
F. W. Street

431   Thank you God for sending Him: thank you God for
           everything.
           J. R. Anderson

432   God is great, God is good: and we thank him for our food.
           Amen.

433   Inner Victory

O Holy Spirit of God, inspirer of all that is good and
beautiful and true in life, come into our hearts this day and
fill us with your light and strength. Help us to hate all sin and
selfishness, and to fight against them with unfaltering courage
and resolve. And because we are weak, and cannot prevail
without your help, strengthen us and give us the victory for
Christ's sake.   Amen.
Harold E. Evans

434   The Present Day

O God our Father, help us today to live as true men. Help us
to do our work as Christ did, putting duty before pleasure,
others before self, and none before you.   Amen.
Harold E. Evans

435   O God, give us cheerfulness and courage to take up again the
           duty you have appointed for each one of us. In this day of
           opportunity let your Holy Spirit inspire us so that however
           humble or hard our task we may do it with true faithfulness
           and greatness of heart, through Jesus Christ our Lord.   Amen.
           Harold E. Evans

436   Daily Life

Christ has no hands but our hands,
Christ has no feet but our feet,
Christ has no love but our love,
To tell of his goodness,
To heal the world's wounds,
To teach the way of love.

We have hands Lord:
With so many things to do,
With varying skills and a myriad tasks,
But there is always time for you.

We have feet Lord:
they take us to so many different places on widely differing
errands.
Sometimes they are so tired Lord and sore and weary.
But they will still go for you, Lord.

We have love Lord:
Love for our husbands, wives and children,
For our friends and relations,
But not always for the others, Lord –
The lonely, the sick and those in pain.
We have love Lord
For so many good things in life,
Please Lord, give us more love for you.
J. E. Morris

PRAYERS FOR CHILDREN'S SERVICES
437   A Confession

O Lord Jesus Christ,
We confess to you now
The wrong things we have done,
The wrong words we have said,
The wrong in our hearts:
Please forgive us
And help us to live as you want us to.   Amen.
Christopher Idle

438   Other Children Who Are Ill

Lord Jesus Christ
Please be very near to those in hospital
(*especially*——
and anyone else we know).
Help them to get better soon;
Help their families not to worry about them;

And help the doctors and nurses to do their work well.
Amen.
Christopher Idle

439   Lord Jesus, we ask you to help us to remember
That you are our friend and Saviour
Wherever we are, and whatever we do;
Be with us in our work and in our games, our home and our
school, our church and our Sunday School (*and*————)
And help us to love you and trust you every day of our lives.
Amen.
Christopher Idle

440   We thank you, God, for our homes:
Our mothers and fathers, our brothers and sisters
And the others in our family;
For all our friends in the same road (*or across the back street or,
as appropriate, 'in the same block'*).
Help us to love and be friends with all of them;
To have no fighting, no quarrels, no bitter thoughts;
But to behave in such a way that everyone else may be glad
to have us living near them;
In the name of Jesus Christ, whom boys and girls were always
glad to meet.   Amen.
Christopher Idle

441   Travellers

We pray, O God, for all who drive on the roads:
For car and van and lorry drivers;
For those who must go fast in ambulances and fire engines
and police cars;
For those who drive long distances, or all through the night
or on difficult roads.
Bless, too, those who travel in other ways, by land, and air
and sea (*especially those on holiday tomorrow/this week/this
month*).
Keep them safe; guard their ways; and bring them safe home
again; through Jesus Christ our Lord.   Amen.
Christopher Idle

442   A Mission Hospital

Thank you Lord God for your hospital and mission at ————
and for your servants who look after it; thank you too for
those who have told us about the things they need in order to
do their work there; thank you for helping us to give our
money to help meet that need: and accept our gifts as we
bring them to you now. May they help to bring healing and
strength of body, mind and spirit to many people, through
Jesus Christ our Lord.   Amen.
Dick Williams

443   An End of Term Prayer For Schools: Our Holidays

Thank you Lord God for helping us to serve you in our
school this term. Thank you for keeping us safe and well.
Thank you for all we have been taught, and all we have found
out for ourselves. Show us how to use what we have learned
in your service and for the good of all. And thank you too
for the holidays which are starting soon. Help us to be
refreshed by doing different things. Help us to be useful at
home. Keep us safe as we play and keep us safe on the roads.
And may we never stop learning whether we are at home or at
school, and help us to understand that everything we learn
can show us more and more about yourself, our creator, our
Lord and our God.
Dick Williams

444   A Thanksgiving for Jesus

Thank you Lord Jesus for stopping to listen to every sick
person who called out to you; thank you for healing every
sort of sickness there is, for feeding the hungry, for setting
men free, and for raising the dead. Bless all the people all over
the world who are trying to follow your example. Bless those
who are taking food to the hungry people, medicine to sick
people, proper forms of government to nations which do not
have real freedom, and your holy gospel to those whose love
for other people is dead. Bless them, and all the sick, sad, and
lonely people to whom they go, for your dear name's sake. Amen.
Dick Williams

445 An Act of Thanksgiving and Intercession

For these and all your gifts, O Lord
We thank you.
For health, and strength, and life itself,
We thank you.
For our friends, our homes, our families,
We thank you.
For our church and our worship,
We thank you.
For every chance to serve you,
We thank you.
For Jesus Christ our Lord,
We thank you.
And now we pray for all who govern our land,
We ask you to bless them.
For all who minister in our church,
We ask you to bless them.
For all who provide our daily needs,
We ask you to bless them.
For all who do not yet know you,
We ask you to bless them.
For all who are tired, or ill, or lonely,
We ask you to bless them.
Hear these prayers, O Lord our God, for Jesus' sake.
Amen.
Christopher Idle

446 Schools

Lord Jesus Christ, the source of all knowledge and truth, give
to all who teach the spirit of wisdom and understanding, and
grant that all who learn may have a true judgment in all
things, that we might be an upright and God-fearing people,
for your sake. Amen.
M. H. Botting's collection

447 At All Saints Tide

For all the men and women, boys and girls, who love and serve
you,
We thank you God.

For everybody who makes Jesus real to other people,
   We thank you God.
For everyone who has taught about you by the way they think,
the way they act and by what they say,
   We thank you God.
For everyone who helps those who are sick or sad, and for
all those who are brave and patient when things are going
wrong,
   We thank you God.
Dear God may we know you better and better so that we may
love you more and more and serve you with all our hearts,
   Please God hear us.
May we help those in need; may they know that God is real
and that God is love,
   Please God hear us.
May we be friends with you, friends with all your children,
friends with one another:
   Please God hear us.
Dick Williams

Experimental Forms

AN ACT OF INTERCESSION FOR OUR NEIGHBOURHOOD

448 Jesus said,

'I have come that men might have *life* and have it in abundance.'
'When I am in the world I am the *light* of the world.'
'This is my commandment that you *love* one another as I have loved you.'

God our Father, who through your Son Jesus Christ has called us to be ministers of your life, your light and your love: help us to obey this call in the neighbourhood of our church, our homes and our work, that we may be quick to seize occasions of service, and wise to use them with care and skill.
Lord in your mercy
Hear this prayer.
(*A Teacher:*) We, who teach in the schools of this neighbourhood, ask you to give us you love and your understanding of children such as we see in the life and teaching of Jesus Christ; that through our ministry they may be guided into the way that leads to the joy and fulfilment of mature life, which Jesus came to give to us all.
Lord in your mercy
Hear this prayer.
(*A Student:*) Help us, as students, to accept with gratitude and humility your gifts of mind and skill, that the Spirit of Truth may use our studies to enlarge our understanding of your purpose for mankind, and may help us to bear witness to the truth of the gospel.
Lord in your mercy
Hear this prayer.
(*A Housewife:*) We who have the care of homes and families,

179

ask for the grace of patience, insight, and personal
understanding, that in ministering your love to those around
us we may build up in each house a fellowship of unity and
service to reflect the light of your presence in its
neighbourhood.
Lord in your mercy
  Hear this prayer.
(*A nurse or doctor:*)   We pray for all who in their various
callings serve the needs of men and women in sickness or in
old age – especially in the hospitals and institutions of this
neighbourhood. Equip us as your fellow workers in the
gospel, and strengthen us to share in your ministry of the
wholeness of life.
Lord in your mercy
  Hear this prayer.
(*An industrialist:*)   Help us to carry from here, into the work
in which we are daily engaged, our faith in your concern for
every area of human life, our interest in every person with
whom we have to do and our calling as men and women
commanded to shine as lights in the world.
Lord in your mercy
  Hear this prayer.
(*Vicar:*)   Almighty God who in the fellowship of this parish
has given us a neighbourhood to serve, and has entrusted us
with the gospel of light, the sacraments of life, and the service
of love, renew us with your Spirit, that in worship and in work
we may be true to our profession as the mission of Christ in
this world –
  Where there is hatred, let us give love;
  Where there is injury, let us give pardon;
  Where there is doubt, let us give faith;
  Where there is despair, let us give hope;
  Where there is sadness, let us give joy;
  Where there is darkness, let us give light.
  For your name's sake.   Amen.
C. B. Naylor, after St Francis

AN ACT OF WORSHIP FOR A CHURCH ANNIVERSARY

449 O God
Greater in majesty than man can imagine;
Mightier in power than man can comprehend;
More beautiful in holiness than man may perceive;
More humble in love than man can ever hope;
Further beyond the reach of man's mind than he can know;
Closer to man's heart than he can learn or desire;
God eternal, known to us forever in Jesus:
We worship and adore you in humility and love for ever, and
ever. Amen.

For awakening men's hearts to yourself;
For reconciling men's hearts to yourself;
For drawing men's hearts to yourself;
For binding men's hearts to yourself;
And, by these means, for building your church here on earth,
We worship and adore you, for ever and ever. Amen.

For giving your eternal spirit to frail and mortal men;
For giving us the message of salvation;
For giving us the power to preach the gospel to all nations;
For giving us all we need in order to obey your will and
commandment;
For giving us joy and fulfilment in your service:
We worship and adore you for ever and ever. Amen.

For the history of your people in all ages;
For the richness and diversity of the Christian family;
For the fellowship of the saints in light;
For all the treasures and resources of the Church universal;
For the vision in the Church of your mighty purposes;
And for our place and part in them where we are today:
We worship and adore you for ever and ever. Amen.

For the founding members of this congregation,
For their vision, their obedience, their enterprise,
For their work of faith, their labour of love, and their
patience of hope,

For the fruits of their labours in the hearts of your servants,
And for the joy of the reward into which they have entered,
We worship and adore you for ever and ever.   Amen.

Bless us in this day of opportunity, O Lord;
May our response to your calling today be full and
abundant, glad and free.
Show us where the real need of mankind lies,
Fashion our minds to find the truth,
Strengthen our wills to do your work,
Purify our hearts that we may see your face,
And fulfil our fellowship in service and in praise.
That by your grace and mercy you may be known to us and
to our children
To our neighbours and to all the world
In time and for eternity
Through Jesus Christ,
Whom with the Holy Spirit and with you
We worship and adore in humility and love for ever and ever.
Amen.
Dick Williams

EDUCATION SUNDAY: A LITANY ON THE THEME OF EDUCATION

450 Let us thank God for the education which we have received.
Let us thank him for the opportunities that still exist for us
to increase our knowledge and education. Let us thank God
for the availability of books, for the public libraries and for
the educational programmes of television and radio.
Lord, in your mercy:
> *Hear our prayer*

Let us pray for our local schools (*enumerate*)
Let us pray for the teaching staff, the domestic staff and the
pupils.
Lord, in your mercy:
> *Hear our prayer*

Let us pray for the members of this congregation involved in
matters of education, for those who teach, for those on
managing and governing bodies of schools, and for those

involved in the daily running and organization of schools.
Lord, in your mercy:
Hear our prayer

Let us pray for the universities and colleges of this country.
Let us remember the ferment in the student world, thanking
God for all that is good in this movement and praying that
all that is evil may be purged from it. Let us ask for
forgiveness for our complacency to some of the injustices in
our society about which students so rightly complain. Let us
pray for members of this church who have recently started at
university or college.
Lord, in your mercy:
Hear our prayer

As we remember with thankfulness the tremendous
educational opportunities we enjoy in this country let us pray
for those without such opportunities in the underdeveloped
countries. Let us pray for God's blessing on all literacy
programmes. Let us pray for the Bible societies, Bible
translators, societies for Christian literature, and for other
agencies involved in the distribution of Christian literature
overseas.
Lord, in your mercy:
Hear our prayer

As we pray for the use of Christian literature overseas, let us
pray too for the educational process of teaching men, women
and children about the life of Christ and his claims upon the
lives of men. Let us pray for the teaching and preaching
ministry of this church.
Lord, in your mercy:
Hear our prayer

Let us pray that the increase in knowledge and education
may not make us as individuals, or as a country, intellectually
proud and spiritually barren. Let us pray that the Lord Jesus
Christ may be recognized as the source of all truth. Finally
let us pray that as Christians we may not be afraid of
knowledge and of truth.
Lord, in your mercy:
Hear our prayer
Peter Markby

LEAVING SCHOOL: WE WELCOME NEW FREEDOMS

451 (*Reader:*) The routines of our former life are passing away now. We have outgrown the formal relationships that protected and disciplined us. We leave behind the shelter of the secondary school. And we enter the arena of free society.

(*A prayer:*)
Lord it is your will for us to welcome new freedoms:
We welcome new freedom to embark on a career
Freedom to earn our own money, or train to earn it
Freedom to spend our money or to save it
Freedom to fashion new routines
Freedom to plan leisure
Freedom to bear new responsibilities
Freedom to make fresh meaning out of life.
We welcome new freedom
To grow into the world you have given us,
To travel to the destination you have prepared for us,
To meet and serve the people you have waiting for us.
In the challenge of freedom – Equip us
In the decisions of freedom – Direct us
In the art of freedom – Discipline us
In the dangers of freedom – Protect us
In the raptures of freedom – Steady us
In the life of freedom – Give us joy
In the use of freedom – Grant us wisdom and the long view.
(*Reader:*) In the factory or firm, in college or office,
In hospital or prison, in city or on the land,
In coffee bar, or on the motorway,
In whatever place, in whatever condition:
(*Leavers:*) We are always free to love our neighbour,
We are always free to love God.
(*Reader:*) Let us now praise those who have given us our immediate heritage: those from whom we have learned to speak and walk, to read and write, to think and understand, to know beauty and to see goodness, to learn of the world and to recognize God.
There are those who have taught us, borne our insults, suffered our ignorance.

There are those who have put up with us and carried us,
covered up for us, and forgiven us, believed in us, and even
enjoyed us.
There are those who forced us to work for our own good,
imposed a sense of order and justice into a muddled life;
encouraged us when we were despairing.
There are those who laughed with us and not at us, who
protected us with their understanding when we were under
fire from others.
There are those whom we have taken for granted.
There are those who have allowed us to take gross advantage
of them.
And there are those who happen to love us.
There need not be jealousy and strife between the generations.
Let us know comradeship with those who are older.
And comradeship with those who will come after us, seeing
that we share the same world, and head for the same
destination.

(*John* 16.25–33)

We are in the world, and we shall have trouble:
We are in the same boat and the boat is being rocked;
We are of the same population and the population is
exploding;
We are on the same road, and the road is blocked.
What a world!
21 million people killed in one war.
Everyone still at a loss to know how to turn their enemies into
friends and win their way of life without the threat of nuclear
disaster.
Two-thirds of the world kept hungry.
130 killed every week on British roads.
Now it is our turn to join in:
We shall be responsible too.

(*A prayer for protection*)
To bear this responsibility we shall need your protection,
Lord – the armour plating of your spirit!
O Lord protect us

From the big businessmen who see us as industrial fodder
From the slick salesmen who treat us as easy market for
industrial junk
From the glib advertisements that promise success for the
price of a tube of toothpaste
From the pressure of unscrupulous competition, from the
status symbol, and the hankering lust for money and
position
From those who would foul our mind, soil our bodies and
ignore our spirits
From the world, the bomb, the drug and the road crash
From ourselves, for we are often our own worst enemy.

(*John* 8.31–36)

What, free to suffer? Yes but to bear it and make meaning
out of it.
What, free to stand the relentless din and monotony of the
factory? Yes, but not to be dehumanized by it.
What, free to take interminable exams? Yes, but not to be
victimized by them.
What, free to be involved in the sins of mankind? Yes but to
be forgiven by the One upon whom the judgment fell.
What, free to believe in a true God of love in a world of
ruin? Yes but not without proving him true.
What, free to die? Yes, but only to find that you are sons and
daughters of God and meant for eternity.
Against all the victimization of the world the Son has set us free
And we are free indeed.
So in the freedom of the Son, the perfect Man,
We shall make money honestly,
We shall make love honourably,
We shall make time for those who need us,
We shall make friends of our enemies,
We shall make amends straight away,
We shall make him supreme,
For his service in the world is perfect freedom.
The Lord is my employer. I shall never be redundant.
Paul Kimber
St Alban's and District Council of Churches

PRAYERS FOR A WOMEN'S SERVICE

452 I was glad when they said unto me, 'Let us go into the house of the Lord.'
Almighty Father
While we are all together in your house we want to thank you for one another.
Please forgive us for the times when we have not loved one another as we love ourselves.
Help us to make the same allowances for another's faults as we do for our own, because we want to be a really loving family, for our Lord's sake.   Amen.
Patricia Mitchell

453 Members of Families

Jesus said 'Let the children come to me...'
We want to thank you Father for all the little children in our family. May we, like you, never be too tired to see and hear them, whenever they need us.
We thank you Lord.   Amen.
Patricia Mitchell

454 His mother said: 'Son why have you treated us so?'
Father we ask you to bless our teenagers. Help us to treat them tenderly; to recognize their need to express themselves; to challenge them, through our own lives, to follow you.
We thank you, Lord.   Amen.
Patricia Mitchell

455 He was welcomed into the house of Martha and Mary.
Father, some of us are like Mary, and some are like Martha. Make us a happy combination of the two, that we may wait upon you with our hands and our hearts.
We thank you, Lord.   Amen.
Patricia Mitchell

456 Ruth said: 'Where you go, I will go...'
For those of us who are committed to caring for a parent,

make us wholehearted in our devotion. Free us from all
strain and stress. Fill us with your peace.
   We thank you, Lord.   Amen.
Patricia Mitchell

457   Lydia, a business woman, opened her heart to Paul's words
and insisted that they stayed at her house.
Father, as we open our hearts to you, may we also open our
homes, giving a warm welcome to all and sharing our faith.
   We thank you, Lord.   Amen.
Patricia Mitchell

458   Anna, a widow of eighty-four, prayed day and night. She
recognized the infant Christ, and told everyone about him.
Some of us, Lord, have known injury, tragedy, heartbreak.
Our faith has been tested and you have sustained us. We
know that our redeemer lives. And we thank you that through
our everyday life, we can show your love and express our
trust.
   We thank you, Lord.   Amen.
Patricia Mitchell

459   Jesus cured Peter's mother-in-law of fever. At once she got up
and began to see to their needs.
Father, we thank you that we women have been fitted to feed
and clothe, cherish and comfort our families and menfolk.
Please increase our gifts of gentleness and healing, that we may
fulfil our role as peacemakers.
   We thank you, Lord.   Amen.
Patricia Mitchell

A SERVICE OF WORSHIP

460   (*1st reader:*)   We have come to worship God our Father: to
acknowledge his power and authority; to give thanks for his
care and his keeping; and to offer ourselves in the service of
Christ. I ask you then to kneel with me and remember God's
presence with us.
(*2nd reader:*)   Almighty God,

Almighty God, our heavenly Father,
We praise and worship you for your goodness, love and mercy;
As Creator of the world, you give us life and breath;
As Preserver of all life, you sustain us day by day;
As Redeemer of mankind, you show forth your love in Christ;
We praise you that the Lord is King, and his Spirit has been
poured into our hearts.
In Christ we join the heavenly host, to praise, to worship and
adore:
Holy, Holy, Holy, Lord God of Hosts!
Heaven and earth proclaim your greatness!
Praise be to your name, O Lord most high!   Amen.

(*A Congregational hymn shall be sung or said*)
(*A Reading*)
(*A Congregational hymn or psalm shall be sung or said or a musical*
or dramatic item may be presented)
(*A Reading*)

(*Intercessions, to which any may contribute:*)
   Lord, we pray for (———) May your will be done
      In this and in all things.

The Lord has heard our prayers;
      And he will answer them.
Let us wait upon the Lord.
      To renew our strength in him.

Then shall follow a period of silence)

Almighty God,
   Almighty God,
   We offer up ourselves to be a living sacrifice,
   Through Jesus Christ our Lord.
   Send us out into the world
   In the power of the Spirit,
   To live and work to your praise and glory.   Amen.
The Lord has sent us forth;
      We will tell his good news to the world.
Giving thanks for his spirit of power,
      We rejoice in his presence both now and for ever.   Amen.
R. C. Thorp

THE MEANING OF IT ALL
Where it all began

461   Hymn: Praise to the Lord, the Almighty
bidding
lesson 1: Creation: Genesis 1.31–2. 3, 21–25
hymn: For the beauty of the earth
lesson 2: A breakdown in human relationships: Genesis 4.1–11
hymn: A charge to keep I have

What God does for us
choir: On Bethlehem's peaceful hill
lesson 3: Hope – in the birth of Jesus: Luke 1.46–55; 2.7
hymn: Christians awake, salute the happy morn, Verses 1, 5
and 6
lesson 4: Jesus is tempted to personal and social evil:
Matthew 4.1–11
choir: Pray for the peace of Jerusalem
lesson 5: Jesus dies – for past, present and future: John 19.23–30
choir: The old rugged Cross
prayer: The Passion of Christ
all sing: (still kneeling): O dearest Lord

Its meaning today
lesson 6: our responsibility: Matthew 25.31–46
folksong: There but for fortune
prayer
lesson 7: faith into practice: James 5.7–20
hymn: Souls of men, why will you scatter

Blessing – Go into the world
hymn: Go tell it on the mountain
St Catherine's church, Wigan

EXHORTATION AND CONFESSION

462   Since none can be pleasing to Almighty God unless his heart
be cleansed from pride through the blood of Christ, and
unless his thoughts, words and actions are directed by the
inner presence of the Holy Spirit; let us kneel before him now
in silence, asking for his grace, mercy and power.   Amen.
Michael Saward

463 If our worship is to be truthful, we must speak, and sing, and hear the truth about God – in the Bible, in our hymns, and in the preaching of the gospel. We need to recognize the truth about one another, and to share our common needs in our prayers together. But first we must admit the truth about ourselves.

We are in the presence of God who knows and examines our hearts, our minds, and our motives. Sin has made us law-breakers in need of pardon, patients in need of healing, and weaklings in need of a new power.

So let us kneel and confess our sin to God.

Christopher Idle

464 **Confession**

Our merciful Father and God, we have wandered from your way, following our own ways. We have ignored the things we should have done and have done things we should not have done. We are just not good enough. We are truly sorry for our failure and humbly claim your promise to forgive us, as declared and demonstrated by our Lord Jesus Christ. We pray, Father, for his sake that we may from now on live a godly, law abiding and sensible life to the glory of your name. Amen.

YOUNG PEOPLE'S SERVICE

465 **Exhortation, Confession, Absolution**

(Call to repent)

Dear fellow Christians, the Gospel urges us, whoever we are, to admit our many sins and shortcomings, and not to try to hide them from Almighty God. Instead we must acknowledge them with humility and obedience, because if we do this he in compassion will forgive us. We should, of course, always admit our sins to God, but never more so than when we meet together to worship him, to give thanks to him for all he has done for us, to listen to his holy Word, and to ask him to meet our needs of soul and body.

I therefore implore you to join me in sincerity and humility, as we say together:

(*General Confession*)

Merciful Father, we have wandered from your paths like sheep; we have often put our own enjoyment first, we have broken your holy laws, we have neglected to do the right, and we have persisted in doing wrong and there is no good in us. Have mercy on us, Lord, sinful though we are. Spare us, O God, as we confess our sins, remake us who are truly sorry; we ask this because of the promises of Christ. Help us, heavenly Father, now to live godly and righteous lives to the glory of your name.   Amen.

(*God's pardon*)

God does not delight in the death of a sinner, but longs for him to abandon his evil ways and live. God has also commanded his ministers with authority to tell those people who are repentant that they are released from their sins. He forgives those who really regret their sin and whole-heartedly believe his holy Word. Let us, therefore, ask God to give us true humility and his Holy Spirit to help us to please him by our actions, and to keep our lives in the future free from sin, so that we may come to his eternal joy, through the grace of his Son Jesus Christ.   Amen.

466   Exhortation, Confession, Absolution

(*Exhortation*)

The word of God urges us to confess to him all the evil that is in us. It urges us not to try to hide these things from God, but to confess them with a heart full of humility and penitence, so that he in his endless mercy, may forgive us. This is something we ought to be doing at all times, but we should surely do it especially when we meet together to thank God for what he has done for us, to praise him, and to hear his word. So come with me now to God's throne of grace, and let us confess our sins together.

(*Confession*)

Almighty and merciful Father, we admit that we have wandered from your way like lost sheep. We have gone according to our own desires and against your laws. We have done things we should not have done, and we have ignored things we should have done. There is

*nothing good about us. But, Lord, show us mercy, spare those who
sincerely confess their faults and restore those who long to be right
with you. For you promised to do this in Jesus Christ. And, Lord,
for his sake, enable us to live from now on a godly and upright life
that will bring honour to your holy name.   Amen.*

(*Absolution*)
All you who have humbly confessed your sins before
Almighty God, be strengthened in faith, remembering that he
does not want even the vilest sinner to die, but would rather
have him turn from his evil ways and live; but God has
commanded his ministers to declare the forgiveness of their
sins to all who truly turn to him. Rest assured therefore, that
your sins have been forgiven through his Son, our Saviour
Jesus Christ, and worry no longer, but let God set your minds
at rest. Amen.

A GENERAL CONFESSION
467   **What's Gone Wrong?**

What's gone wrong? *We* have, Lord, every day of our life, in
failing to fulfil our responsibilities. So, Lord, for hasty words
we utter, thoughtless actions we do, unloving thoughts which
cross our minds day by day, and which break up our
fellowship
    Please forgive
For failing to listen sympathetically when people are talking
to us about their troubles
    Please forgive
For failing to give up time which is precious to others when
they need our love
    Please forgive
For losing opportunities to teach our families about Christ,
moral standards, and life in general
    Please forgive
For failing to search out the troubles and needs of others
For being satisfied within ourselves when so many are in
moral danger, dying of hunger, both spiritual and physical,

and many do not know about Christianity
Please forgive
For failing to put God first in our own lives
Please forgive
O Lord, we come before you humbly, asking for your
forgiveness for these and other faults we have. Give to us we
pray, your Holy Spirit to lead us more and more into lives
which show outwardly the love of yourself in Jesus Christ our
Lord. Amen.
Bob Metcalfe

PREPARATION FOR HOLY COMMUNION

468 Give us the grace, our Father, to judge ourselves before we
are judged by you; to repent truly for past sin; to have a
lively and steady faith in Christ our Saviour; and to be willing
to live more faithfully to you from now on.
You sent your Son to give himself for us; may we prove our
love by giving ourselves to you, and serving you for his sake
every day of our life. Amen.
Christopher Idle (based on Book of Common Prayer Exhortation)

FOR GRACE

469 O God our Father, we thank you that tonight you have called
us to worship you and learn of you. You alone know our
needs. Satisfy them with your unchanging love. In your
presence may we find comfort in sorrow, guidance in
perplexity, strength to meet temptation, grace to overcome
the fascination of disobedience, and courage to face up to the
hostility of this rebellious world. Above all, may we meet Jesus
and go out from our worship indwelt by his spirit. This prayer
we ask to your glory and in his name. Amen.
Michael Saward

THE LORD'S PRAYER

470 Heavenly Father, may your name be precious to us; may your
authority rule the earth as it does in heaven; and swiftly bring
your kingdom here.

Provide for us in our daily needs, we pray. Please forgive us
all that we have done against you, in as much as we forgive
those who have wronged us. Help us to stay clear of the things
that make us sin, and the evil that lies behind them; because
we pray in the name of Jesus.   Amen.

CHRISTMAS
471   Act of Penitence

Sorry, full up! No room here!
Not a hope! Go away!

Lord, we remember that when you first came to earth there
was no room for you.

No one spared a thought for the condition of your mother;
No one thought of anyone but themselves.

The world hasn't changed much, Lord:
Human nature hasn't changed much either.

Lord, forgive our unwillingness to find a place for you in our
crowded lives.

Forgive our love of self which sees our wellbeing as all
important.

Forgive our corporate neglect of the homeless, the
destitute, the under-privileged, the unfortunate, who like you
have nowhere to lay their heads.

> *Lord, forgive what we have been, amend what we are, direct
> what we shall become, for the sake of Jesus Christ our Lord.
> Amen.*
> Gordon Bates

ACT OF INTERCESSION

472   Born of Jewish parentage
Under Roman rule
Worshipped by the Orient
Lord, all are one in you.

Bring this fact home to our world, Lord – that all men are equal and of great importance to you.

Give peace among the nations of the world, that men may come to love and not to hate each other.

Take from us and from our world
all prejudice of colour, class and creed.

Bring justice and right dealing in situations where men are oppressed.

And for ourselves we pray Lord use us as instruments of your peace...

> *Where there is war, may we work for peace:*
> *where there is despair, may we bring hope:*
> *where there is suspicion and hatred, may we sow the seeds of*
> *love and trust:*
> *and as our lives are filled with your life-giving Spirit, may we, in*
> *our day, work to build up the Kingdom of your Son, Jesus*
> *Christ our Lord.   Amen.*

Gordon Bates

DO I FAIL MY NEIGHBOUR?

473 When I go home and sit down to a good meal
>   *Do I fail my neighbour?*

When I am fully clothed and look for more to fill my wardrobe
>   *Do I fail my neighbour?*

When I go and buy unnecessary luxuries for myself
>   *Do I fail my neighbour?*

When I shrink from listening sympathetically, and from teaching my children about Jesus and his way of life
>   *Do I fail my neighbour?*

When I care only for my family and leave others to care for themselves
>   *Do I fail my neighbour?*

When I gloat about my own life, which I think is good
>   *Do I fail my neighbour?*

God says:

Yes, my child, and I, your God, your Father, am angry with

you. I gave you the world at the beginning of time, and I
want each of my sons to be worthy of their Father in my vast
Kingdom.
I trusted you, and your selfishness has spoiled everything.
It is one of your most serious sins, shared by many of you.
Woe unto you, if, through your fault, a single one of my sons
dies in body or spirit. The thoughtless, the negligent, the
selfish, those who are well-sheltered on earth, who have
forgotten others, they have had their reward, and there will be
no room for them in my Kingdom.

Come, ask forgiveness for yourself and others tonight. And
tomorrow, fight with all your might, and with all your
strength, for it hurts your Father to see once more, there is no
room for his Son at the Inn.
I will say no more now, go out, get on with it, and my
blessing will be with you.
Bob Metcalfe

MEDITATION
474   I Thought I Could Get By, Lord

Whenever I worried over my job, which I did frequently;
Whenever I had arguments at home – we got over them;
Whenever I saw sickness and, indeed, when I was once very
ill myself – and got better;
Whenever I watched the TV and saw fighting, always at a
distance;
Whenever I attended the funeral of a friend, and I realized
that it wasn't my own;
Whenever friends let me down, and I always managed to find
a new one;
It was then –
I thought I could get by, Lord.

As I was able to earn good money at work, or pick up good
money when out of work;
As I never went short of food or clothing;
As I enjoyed my family, my wife and children, and am a
happily married man;

As I derived plenty of pleasure from the local club;
As I relaxed in the garden, motoring or watching the
television;
As I realized that I'd got everything I want;
Nothing ever really bothered me, so
I thought I could get by, Lord.

The people told me that I needed Jesus Christ, and I saw the
Church;
I heard them talk of God inside the building, but never
outside as if they meant it;
I couldn't understand their language, and their services were
deadly dull;
I listened to words about Christian joy, but I was just as happy
as they were;
I observed the church members squabbling amongst themselves
more than I did at home, and I didn't want to share in their
pettiness;
I saw Northern Ireland and the trouble caused there because
of religious differences;
I was told to be good and caring towards others, but I can do
that without going to church;
It's no wonder, is it
I thought I could get by, Lord?

Then
I saw myself
Growing older, greyer, and less active than once I was.
I wondered, I wondered, Lord –
Who am I?
What am I doing here?
Was there something else?
How long will it go on, and then what will happen?
No one could tell me, Lord, until you said:
My dear child, you think you can get by without me.
You are wrong.
Yet, wrong as you are, I love you and my love has touched
your heart at last before it is too late.
Jesus was my Love as he suffered for you – and died.
He has shown what my love means because he rose, and came

to be with me in heaven.
My love is now my Spirit within you.
That love will bring you and others to me;
Without me you are lost.
Don't be lost.
Come, and keep coming, to me.
Bob Metcalfe

JUST YOU AND JESUS

475 'Stretch out your love to Jesus Christ. You have won him!
Touch him with as much love as you sometimes feel for a
man' (Ancrene Riwle).
We are together before God.
We are alone before God.
We need each other
But we also need to be alone.
So together but in silence
We will seek God.
Everyone in his own way
Let us talk to him.
Let us listen to him.
Let us look at him face to face.
Let us touch him if we can,
Alone and yet together.

You are beautiful, my beloved, truly lovely[1]
With great delight I sat in his shadow[2]
My beloved is mine and I am his.[3]
I found him whom my soul loves.[4]
Love is strong as death.[5]
Many waters cannot quench love.[6]   Amen. Amen. Amen.
Simon H. Baynes

WEEKEND WORLD

476 We come from the fish shop, the café, the corner, the
motorway.
This is the world we have made, we admit it –

From the Song of Solomon [1]1.16,   [2]2.3,   [3]2.16,   [4]3.4,   [5]8.6,   [6]8.7.

The betting shop and the bingo hall, the pub and the
bowling lanes.

It is he that has made us, and not we ourselves
Good or bad, we can hardly tell. He knows
The sins we commit are never wholly bad;
Our good deeds are usually tainted.
Where do we go from here?

We are the sheep of his hand
Some of our ways look shady. In the back street, at the side
door
God knows what we talk about on the street corner.

All the corners of the earth are in his hand
And so we admit that God is all in all.
We cannot escape him, we cannot ignore him.
Somehow we trust that you, our God, are here and now,
Present in this wandering weekend world.
Present in all the beauty and ugliness around us
With us here and now and for ever.

Come on, let's worship, and kneel before the Lord our
Maker.

(*To be followed by a time of silent worship.*)
Simon H. Baynes

WHEN WE FORGET GOD

477 The Glory of Israel will not lie or repent.
He is not a man that he should repent.[1]
He changes not.[2]
Can a woman forget her sucking child? Even these may
forget, yet I will not forget you.[3]
Jesus Christ is the same yesterday and today and forever.[4]

Unchangeable God, we so easily forget.
Much of our lives we live as though you were not there.
We rest in the certainty that you never forget us.
And so at the same time we confess and give thanks,
We sorrow and rejoice.

[1] 1 Samuel 15.29;   [2] Malachi 3.6;   [3] Isaiah 49.15;   [4] Hebrews 13.8.

Can we not find you in forgetting religious things?
Can we not find you in finding others?
Can we not find you in losing ourselves in our work?
So in losing may we find,
And in forgetting, remember.
Give us the grace to find you, changeless Lord,
The Glory of Israel, in forgetting ourselves.
Give us the mind to love our neighbours as ourselves.

As you did it to one of the least of these my brethren, you
did it to me.[1]
Simon H. Baynes

LIFE, LIFE!

478   'Then the man put his fingers in his ears and ran on crying
"Life, life, eternal life!" So he looked not behind him but fled
towards the middle of the plain.' (*Pilgrim's Progress.*)

Before it is too late
We come to pray for life.
We meet in the presence of the living God.
'In him was life'.[2]

We meet in the presence of Jesus
Who lived as no one else has lived.
Jesus, who died a young man,
We long for life to the full;
We need your spirit today.
We need your spirit of abandon.
'The life was the light of men'.[3]

God, enliven us.
God, wake us up.
God, save us from half life, half truths, white lies.
'I am the bread of life'.[4]

Lord and giver of life, we pray
So come to us
That we may be like dead men
Struck by lightning, born again

[1] Matthew 25.40;   From John's Gospel   [2]1.4,   [3]1.4,   [4]6.35.

Alive to God,
Alive to others
Alive to our best selves,
Before it is too late
'I came that they might have life.'[1]

That we may not waste our best years
Going the way of the world
Falling short of the glory of God
With double minds and divided hearts
We acknowledge that we are needy beyond measure
And the way of Jesus is the only way.
'I am the way, the truth and the life'.[2]
Amen, Amen, Amen.
Simon H. Baynes

THE LOVE THAT GETS US

479   God, what power! It's like a live thing inside us.

We are fearfully and wonderfully made

What are we to do, God, when the body takes control?
It's like a wild animal that suddenly takes charge.

Man was made in the image of God.

A wild animal, but beautiful too.
We don't see much beauty in the world around us.
This is like nothing on earth. God, what are we to do?
This is the first commandment...

God, we don't want any more of that.
The whole world is grey with commandments
But this – it's like switching the TV over to colour.
It's like a new world. God, can it really be wrong?

This is the first commandment,
Thou shalt love the Lord thy God.

Yes, Lord our God, we do try to, in our humble way.
But it seems a long stretch, a far cry from all this, here and
now.

[1] John 10.10,   [2] 14.6.

God, we love you, but you are so far away.

There is a mediator between God and man, the man Christ
Jesus.
Jesus, yes Jesus is great too, we love him as we can; but
somehow it's different for us; here we are in this swinging
world,
And this thing goes through us like an electric shock...

In all points tempted as we are, yet without sin.
In all points, Lord our God, yes perhaps we had forgotten.
In all points. Yet without sin.
So it means an iron resolution,
An all-out effort of self-control...

The second commandment...

Yes God, no need to tell us, we know only too well.
It's 'thou shalt not' all along the line.

Thou shalt love...

Love?

Thou shalt love thy neighbour...

That's just the trouble God;
Sometimes even the girl next door...

Thou shalt love thy neighbour as thyself.

As myself?
As myself. As myself.
Now I think I begin to understand.
Thank you, God.
Simon H. Baynes

THANK GOD FOR THAT

480   Lord God of heaven and earth,
We have to admit we find it hard to praise.
It is hard to be always dependent.
Our thanksgiving rings a little hollow.
We cannot be children for ever.

Give thanks to the Lord for he is good.

We are not ungrateful, but we expect our due.
The bread we bought today we earned yesterday.
How can we pray 'give us our daily bread'?
It comes from the baker's, not like manna from heaven.

The earth is the Lord's

The earth is yours, Lord, but you have given it to man.
It is ours to discover and use and work to the full
All the marvels of science are in the hands of man.
We believe that science is your gift and your will for us.
We are indeed grateful for this power.
We thank you for growth and health and life itself.

In everything give thanks.

Lord, you understand us.
It is hard to be thankful for every little thing.

In everything give thanks.

But for *everything*...

In everything.

In everything.
Yes Lord. So in fullness, and in loneliness,
In times of depression, in the hour of love,
In moments of great blessing, in our boredom, in our dreams,
In business, at weekends, and on Monday mornings,
In everything we will give thanks.
Simon H. Baynes

AN ACT OF SUPPLICATION
481   Crying out for Power – All Power Belongs to God.[1]

We remember and are thankful.
At the same time we marvel and are afraid
At the power given to man.

[1] Psalm 62.11.

Power to touch the stars,
To heal a man's mind or break his spirit,
To make or break this world,
To transplant life; almost to create.

All power belongs to God.

Let us then remember O Lord
our childishness.
Let us take power from your hands
with awe, as creatures,
not with pride as usurpers.

Let us glorify God, who has given such power to man.[1]

Let us beware of asking for more responsibility than we can
bear.
The world is crying out for more power.[2]
But we will remember weakness,
Our own and another's.
We renounce all power that is not from God.

All power belongs to him.

We remember that the place of salvation was a place of
torture
Where a man could not move hand or foot to help himself,
and had nothing to call his own.

Though he was crucified in weakness,
Yet he lives by the power of God.[3]

Saviour Jesus, take your own power and live and reign
among us.
Simon H. Baynes

WHEN YOU FEEL LIKE SINGING

482   Something in us is making music.
Something in us wants to dance.
Something makes us want to sing.

---

[1] Matthew 9.8.   [2] Caption of an advertisement for electric power.
[3] 2 Corinthians 13.4.

Sing a new song to the Lord.[1]

Lord, it's you we should be praising,
Like a father, the best we can think of.
Lord, you're the best of anything we know.

Sing a new song to the Lord.

We hardly know, Lord, how things started.
There was a great voice, and a great light
There was a great power, it's all a great mystery.

But the morning stars sang together
And the sons of God shouted for joy.[2]

We are grateful for all the music of life,
The sea's roar, the song of a well-tuned engine
The silvery beauty of Mendelssohn
The red-hot rhythm of jazz.

Let the morning stars sing together,
And the sons of God shout for joy!

Better than these is the song inside us
Because it is our own, coming from our hearts.
We sing because we are grateful, we praise because we love.

Sing a new song to the Lord.
So here we are, Lord, with a new song to sing you.
We are not very clean; we all have mixed motives,
We are not very strong, and often fall
But we come with love, which is all we can boast of,
And a new song; Lord make us new.

Sing a new song to the Lord.
Simon H. Baynes

STARVING MILLIONS, SO WHAT?

483 God give hearts.
We want to admit we come of a heartless world.
Pictures of starving children hardly give us a qualm.
The appeals for charity leave us cold.

[1] Psalm 96.1;   [2] Job 38.7.

I will take away your heart of stone.[1]

Thank you for the promise, God of promises.
Can it be true?
At the moment we are set on getting all sorts of things
It's a hard thing we are asking you to do.
We give to a charity, but as a duty.
We never feel what we think we ought to feel.

I will give you a heart of flesh.[2]

Lord make the promise good. We claim it now.
Take our heartless lives, our so-called loves and our
ambitions.
We are asking for a miracle. We pray for love.

I will put my spirit in you.[3]

God, we believe it.
Come, Lord Jesus.
Come, Holy Spirit.

They were all filled with the Holy Spirit.[4]

Spirit of Jesus, lead us to the truth.
Spirit of God, open our eyes to see
Not starving millions, but a child without food
Not malnutrition, but a man dying before his time.

Once I was blind but now I see.[5]

Thank God for his gift which is beyond all words.[6]
Simon H. Baynes

484 Son of man, Jesus Christ, we remember your commands.

Be wise as serpents.[7]
Be experts in goodness.[8]
In understanding be men.[9]

Make us men, unsentimental, hard-headed, practical.

[1] Ezekiel 11.19; [2] Ezekiel 36.26; [3] Ezekiel 36.27; [4] Acts 2.4; [5] John 9.25;
[6] 2 Corinthians 9.15; [7] Matthew 10.16; [8] Romans 16.19; [9] 1 Corinthians 14.20.

We have a problem and we bring it to you, Jesus Christ son
of man.
The world you have made is broken in half.
Half starved.
Half forgotten.
Man Jesus Christ, what do you want us to do?
Tell us now,
What can we do as single Christians?

They first gave their own selves to the Lord.[1]

What can we do as families?

I was a stranger and you took me in.[2]

Go into all the world and preach the gospel to every
creature.[3]

Church, home, self.
Time, interest, understanding.
Money.
Son of man, what you have freely given, we give back.
Show us how. Show us how much.
Turn our words into action. Man Jesus, make us men.
Simon H. Baynes

MY DESK

485   My desk. School again after the holidays.
Ugh...Must get a desk next to Mary.
I like to sit near the front – but not too near.
The best place is near the radiator if you can get it.
Not a bad form room this.
Desk inspection soon, I suppose – better get the books put
in tidily.
There now – we're all ready for the new year.
I always feel I'm going to do better than last year.
Something a bit exciting about a new school year – though it
doesn't do to admit it.

My desk. I remember a missionary from India came to talk to
us last year.

[1] 2 Corinthians 8.5; [2] Matthew 25.35; [3] Mark 16.15.

She said she hadn't enough desks in her school for all the children.
Parents begged for their children to be allowed to have desks in the corridors
So that with the door open, they would gather a few crumbs.
Countless children in the world never even have the chance to read and write.
It seems unbelievable.
I shall learn a second language this year.
Miss Shaw says my writing is deplorable
But I can write quite nicely if I really take the trouble.

Funny to think my desk is something millions of children would like to have.

We thank you, Lord, for all those who have taught us
With patience and understanding.
We remember all who have never had the chance to go to school
We thank you for the ability to study and make progress.
We thank you for this school
And for all our opportunities for work and leisure.
K. A. Clegg

MY HOME

486   Aren't parents difficult sometimes?
You should have heard the row we had last night.
What was it this time?
Oh – they said I stayed out too late –
They were worried sick – the usual thing.
Have you ever longed for a little flat on your own?
Yes – you bet – but to be honest I think I'd be lonely sometimes.
Yes, I expect you're right. There is something special about belonging to a family.
I know; I realize we're very lucky really to have parents who bother about us.
And after all, if parents *are* difficult, I expect we are too.

Let us give thanks to God for our homes and families and

pray that we may grow in appreciation of all that we have been given in love and material blessings over the years.

May we be kept from treating our homes as lodging houses and from showing insufficient concern for our parents. As we thank God for our homes we pray for all the homeless throughout the world.

We remember the homeless in this country and the work of Shelter.

We think of all the refugees – keep their distress in our minds – it is so easy for 'refugee' to become just a word to us.

We make this prayer in the name of Jesus who lived in a family in Nazareth.

K. A. Clegg

Index

(Numbers refer to prayers, not pages.)

(R) after a prayer number denotes a Responsive prayer.
This is an *additional* Index; in the main, subjects have not been indexed which
are a distinct section and shown in the Contents list at the front of the book,
in conjunction with which this should be used.